STRANGE GUESTS

BY BRAD STEIGER

ANOMALIST BOOKS
*San Antonio * New York*

CONTENTS

FOREWORD

THE BOOK YOU HOLD in your hands is a special treat. This text by Brad Steiger and introduction by Ivan T. Sanderson is a rare event in publishing on the subject of the unexplained. Here you have two celebrated writers trying to tackle one of the major mysteries of humankind–poltergeists. If you are not familiar with these two masters of the unknown, let me introduce them to you.

Brad Steiger was born in Fort Dodge, Iowa, in 1936, and went on to be a creative writing professor at a small college in Iowa. Steiger's first published articles on the unexplained appeared in 1956. Since then he has authored or coauthored 160 books on subjects ranging from UFOs to werewolves with more than 17 million copies in print. Steiger is now recognized worldwide as an authority on the strange and unknown.

Ivan T. Sanderson was born in Edinburgh, Scotland, in 1911, and after World War II he moved to the United States and became a naturalized citizen. Leading expeditions to the jungles of the world, even as a teenager, the biologist and zoologist also appeared on the early Gary Moore-hosted Today Show as television's first "animal man." He wrote on many cryptozoological subjects (and even coined the term) as well as about unknowns generally labeled "Fortean," after the 1920s' American intellectual Charles Fort who was passionate about subjects that science excluded and "damned." Sadly, Sanderson passed away from cancer on February 19, 1973, his work unfinished, but his legacy intact.

Through poltergeists and this book, you will find that Steiger and Sanderson have indeed captured, as best they could, that weird and intangible phenomenon of the poltergeists. I too have been drawn to the subject of poltergeists. Sanderson once convinced me that of all psychic phenomena, poltergeists was the one that stood the best chance of being proven. Here we have a type of ghost that bangs around, touches people, and leaves traces. It may not be an animal, but it certainly seems to be more measurable than anything else in the paranormal, and as such the phenomenon represents a gap in our knowledge.

But neither Steiger nor Sanderson have let this gap in our knowledge stop them, for the data is there and the cases exist. *Strange Guests* presents some of the best cases in support of these "noisy ghosts." Enjoy the adventure.

Loren Coleman
Author of *Mysterious America*
Portland, Maine
August 1, 2006

INTRODUCTION

It used to be that the question "Do you believe in ghosts" was employed as a stopper in argument, debate, or just plain conversation. Its employment was equivalent to that of short-range mortar fire. It brought your opponent to a thundering stop and usually annihilated him mentally because it implied that he was capable of believing anything and therefore unfit for intellectual society. But times have changed.

The question is now used as a gentle probe to ascertain whether your opponent *is* capable of believing in anything—other than what everybody else believes in, that is.

Of course, what to believe in and what not to believe in today presents a pretty problem. For instance, there may be one or two left who still steadfastly refuse to believe in sputniks on the grounds that we have not got one in the Smithsonian where it may be measured and weighed. On the other hand, there is hardly any diminution of the numbers who believe in the Holy Ghost. We used to believe things on faith; now we are coming, and most happily, to demand facts before we make up our minds. This can, of course, go too far, as in the case of sputniks, but this is due to an inability—often inborn—to assess evidence and, were it not for tracking and detection devices, it would indeed be hard for the average person to prove to himself the existence of sputniks.

Ghosts in the generic sense constitute a most excellent subject for intellectual exercise and debate, and they should form an important field for scientific enquiry. They are particularly worthy because there is one genus among them that is just as amenable to detection and tracking as any sputnik and in some cases even more so. It is the old saw about electricity. Nobody has seen it but from observing what it does, we have found out what it is and how it works. With some species of ghosts

7

it works even better, provided you will accept certain categories of evidence, for it is alleged that "it" (they) can be seen. The genus of ghost that we can really get our hands on, as it were, is the *Poltergeist*.

The name *ghost* has a most interesting origin. The Germans pronounce it and spell it *geist,* an expression derived from the old Norse *geisa* which meant "rage" or "fury," which came out in early Gothic as *us-gais-jan,* meaning "to terrify." It is perhaps interesting to note that these things enraged the good old, self-sufficient, pagan Nordmanni but terrified the early Christians. And herein lies a clue. Ghosts, and particularly poltergeists just didn't fit into the Christian ethos. They are an affront to our beliefs at any time, but there were particularly outrageous to the Christian concept of life and creation. They did not fit into it; they smacked of the Devil, and this scared the daylights out of everybody, and still continues to do so. Among peoples of other faiths, please note, this is not the case; they are accepted and, in some cases, as among the Malayan peoples, they occupy their own somewhat honored niche in the overall scheme of things.

Geists are apparently a vast host of wildly assorted forms of "life." That they are animate as opposed to inanimate is manifest by the things they *do.* It is very hard, if not impossible, to define "life" or draw a line between the animate and the inanimate but there are innumerable things that what we call living entities do that stones, for instance, have never been known to do, and it is just such things that are perpetrated by these *Poltergeists.*

By definition, a poltergeist is a geist that throws things; but that's not the half of it. There are stinkergeists, howlergeists, literary geists, funny geists, and damned-nuisance if not downright dangerous geists. And, I am not talking about plain haunts and other species detectable only by sight. As you will learn by reading on, poltergeists do the darnedest things—things, moreover, that *can* be measured or otherwise detected, as by photography. These things happen, so it is quite useless saying they don't. As to what causes them, nobody yet knows for sure but, as the doing of them calls for the output of energy, one can only assume that within the framework of our present logic and accepted physical laws there is some force in operation. This has been tagged poltergeist. That is all there is to it.

The line of demarcation between plain ordinary ghosts and poltergeists is doubtless manmade. They probably blend one into the other category but one has to draw the line somewhere, and said empirical line lies between those which are allegedly only felt or seen on the one hand, and those which produce physical effects, on the other. If you ever got a good movie of the first category it would presumably pop over into the second.

The first category is very difficult and happily not the purlieu of this book. How are we to record what people see or feel? We can see them shaking with fright; we can measure heartbeats and perhaps even adrenalin output, but all such manifestations may be brought on by the persons themselves and even be wholly of what we call the mind. In fact, the current explanation for ghosts is that they are of a psychological nature, using that word in its widest sense. And, stemming from this belief, psychologists have invaded the provinces of the poltergeist.

Since poltergeists "do things" of a physical nature that can not be denied, it has been suggested that these "things" are subconscious or unconscious actions on the part of people by the employment of innate forces which all or some of us possess, but the nature of which we do not yet understand. There is no doubt that on many occasions poltergeist manifestations center around, occur only in the presence of, and follow certain persons about. There are now thousands of documented cases of this nature, from keys jumping out of door locks in a crowded hospital ward, to water and gasoline pouring out of dry wells in farmhouses—manifestations which went along with a patient when moved to another ward and a teenage girl when moved to a distant homestead. But here comes the rub.

Are these people the poltergeists themselves, or are they acting like radios, receiving and then broadcasting directed energies from some other source?

You can debate that one forever but one thing you can be sure of and this is that it is not the whole or only answer. Poltergeist manifestations may also be attached to places or objects and can operate without anybody being present. Of this sort of thing you will read plenty anon, and it is really rather disturbing. Finally, they need not be attached to anything but just happen. These are the most aggravating of all.

Poltergeist manifestations display an enormous range of both procedure and result. Some appear to be purely mechanical, like stones materializing in a lighted room and dropping slowly to the floor. Other times we are forced to the conclusion that they are the deliberate actions of an intelligence of fairly high order. Very few ever appear logical, though many seem to us to be mischievious and aggravating. Strangely, they are very seldom dangerous or harmful, and they often seem to take pains not to be. A group of State Police investigating a continuous hail of stones in a California case recently noted especially that, while their cars were hit and dented occasionally, they themselves were never touched.

When reading this book, then, don't hide it under the pillow or from your friends. I know this used to be a subject for much ribbing and one that, if you showed signs of taking it seriously, would almost assuredly lay you open to the gravest suspicion of insanity, mysticism, or at least kookery. Take heart: this book is really a pretty advanced scientific study of a most practical nature. True, these are wonderful stories, but so is our entrance into outer space. There is a whole world here for exploration and we now have the tools with which to explore it. Go to it, I say.

IVAN T. SANDERSON
Blairstown, N.J.
1966

HOME IS WHERE THE HAUNT IS

THEY HAD just begun to eat dinner when a miniature pottery pitcher exploded on a dining room shelf.

Edgar Jones pushed his chair back from the table and brushed ceramic fragments off his sleeve and shoulder. "What in blazes caused that?" he asked his wife, who had jumped to her feet with housewifely concern over her collection of pottery pitchers.

"Oh, mother," sighed their daughter, Mrs. Pauls, her surprise changing to sympathy, "that was one of your favorite miniatures, too."

"I'll get a broom and dust pan," Mrs. Jones said, masking her anxiety.

But before she could move, another pitcher exploded. Then another and another, as if an invisible marksman had decided to use the Jones' dining room shelf as a shooting gallery. One by one, each of fifteen tiny pitchers shattered as if it had been pierced by an unseen bullet. The family moved away from the table in bewilderment, their confusion rapidly bordering on fear and panic.

The incident of the exploding pitchers was but the first in a succession of strange and unfathomable phenomena which took place in the Edgar C. Jones family in Baltimore, Ohio, between January 14th and February 8th in 1960.

Once, while the startled family watched, a ceramic flower pot lifted itself from a shelf and crashed out a nearby window pane.

During another meal, a sugar bowl floated up to the chandelier and dumped its contents in the candle holders.

Pictures tumbled off their hooks and crashed to the floor. A brass incense burner flew six feet off a bookshelf.

While Mrs. Jones and Mrs. Pauls prepared an evening

meal, several iced-tea glasses danced off a kitchen shelf, and two ashtrays emptied their refuse on the floor.

A case of soda bottles exploded like a string of firecrackers.

Some pottery pieces left on a bed were smashed by an unseen force. A small table on a stairway landing suddenly became animated and managed a splintering descent of the stairs. A stack of fireplace wood exploded in the basement, sending bits of bark and pulp across the floor like wooden shrapnel.

The dining room chandelier swung violently during most of the meals, and eating utensils often left the table to scatter themselves about the floor. An artificial Christmas tree launched itself several feet in the air, catapulting its ornaments in a shower of brightly-colored missiles.

The only physical harm suffered by any member of the family during that period of domestic outrages was endured by Mr. Jones when he bent to pick up a can of corn that had popped off a shelf. As he stooped to retrieve the corn, a can of sauerkraut toppled and struck him on the head.

The police department's crime laboratory could find no trace of any explosives having been inserted in any of the moving or exploding objects. City highway workmen tested for tremors with a seismograph and found nothing. A radio repairman blamed the trouble on high-frequency radio wave lengths, but his intricate equipment could record none. A local plumber looked for the cause in the hot-air furnace. Reporters, television crews, psychic investigators, and cultists swarmed the house, each with his own theory of the disturbance and his own remedy for "laying" the ghost. The phenomena, however, ceased just as suddenly as it had begun, leaving the Joneses just as baffled as when the first miniature pottery pitcher exploded.

Although the series of eerie events experienced by the Jones family were decidedly unusual, they are by no means unique. Records of such disturbances as these date from as early as 355 A.D. to as recent as this morning's newspaper. Such phenomena is said to be the work of a *poltergeist* (German for *noisy spirit*). Witnesses to poltergeist activity often are highly educated and responsible persons who claim to have seen and heard unexplained sights and sounds—objects that move without any traceable causes, and, in some cases, rappings and voices that exhibit intelligence. Frequently, the poltergeist is unmasked as a combination of trickery and hallucination, intensified by the power of suggestion; but many poltergeist cases have never been satisfactorily explained and remain enigmas that have baffled the best minds of the ages.

The late psychoanalyst, Dr. Nandor Fodor, believed that there was no doubt that the poltergeist was indeed a part of our world of reality. He pointed out that the life-time of a poltergeist was usually limited to a few weeks or months. The poltergeist became, as it were, an unbidden guest, moving in to work its pranks on an unappreciative family. The difference between a ghost and a poltergeist, Dr. Fodor said, is that the ghost haunts a house and the poltergeist haunts a person.

"The poltergeist is not a ghost," Dr. Fodor stated, "but a bundle of projected repressions."

Like the majority of psychical researchers, Dr. Fodor held that poltergeist activity is usually associated with a teen-aged member of a family, more often a girl than a boy. An exhaustive study of poltergeist manifestations convinced noted investigator Harry Price that the sexual change of puberty is frequently associated with either the beginning or the cessation of the phenomena.

Sacheverell Sitwell has written his opinion that the poltergeist finds its center of energy in the person of an adolescent, who performs the effects, both consciously and unconsciously, "being gifted for the time being with something approaching criminal cunning. The particular direction of this power is always towards the secret or concealed weaknesses of the spirit . . . the obscene or erotic recesses of the soul. The mysteries of puberty, that trance or dozing of the psyche before it awakes into adult life, is a favorite playground for the poltergeist."

Dr. Fodor personally investigated the Jones case in Baltimore and concentrated on the Jones's seventeen-year-old grandson, Ted Pauls. A shy, brooding youth, the family told Dr. Fodor that Ted had left school at the

13

legal age because he was so brilliant that classes bored him.

Dr. Fodor later reported: "I found a therapeutic approach to the problem of the poltergeist. The boy had talent that clamored for expression . . ." Dr. Fodor theorized that the mechanics of the poltergeist activity had been accomplished by "psychic dissociation." For the psychoanalyst, this meant that "the human body is capable of releasing energy in a manner similar to atomic bombardments . . . force was apparently able to enter soda bottles that had not been uncapped and to burst them from within."

But most certainly "brain activity" or an intelligence is involved in poltergeist phenomena. On-the-spot investigators, who have witnessed "flying" objects turn corners or pieces of chalk forming crude sentences on walls, are convinced that the activity involves more than an explosive burst of energy. Psychic researchers believe that science must deal with an energy force directed by a measure of intelligence or purpose. One investigator has observed that the phenomena are "exactly such as would occur to the mind of a child or an ignorant person."

The most elementary of the poltergeist's pranks is that of lobbing stones and other small objects. Also near the bottom rung of its repertoire are such relatively simple effects as loud rappings and the sudden appearance of water. A bit higher on the scale is the ability to cause objects to burst into flames. Still higher on the poltergeist's graph of personal achievement is the power to move heavy furniture and to methodically destroy all things breakable. The poltergeist is also quite an accomplished one if it can produce strange lights, disagreeable odors, and eerie sounds. But the ultimate in poltergeistic prowess are the materializations of human and beastlike entities, the productions of voices that converse intelligently with the afflicted members of the household, and the manipulations of writing instruments to effect a record of communication.

The poltergeist at its most proficient produces phenomena that is capable of unnerving the most profound realist and the most rigid skeptic.

THE ENTIRE HOUSEHOLD of Calvados Castle had been disturbed by the strange, midnight noises that had echoed throughout the dark corridors. That morning, the master of Calvados thought that he had the answer to the nocturnal knockings and thumpings.

"Someone is obviously trying to frighten us away from the castle so that they might purchase the surrounding land at a fraction of its value," he announced to his coachman and gardener. "They have no doubt found entrance to the castle by means of some long forgotten passage. They probably think it a simple matter to drive a man away from an old castle that he has just inherited."

He had no sooner finished theorizing when they heard howling and barking from the two formidable watchdogs which he had recently purchased. Rushing to a window, the master of Calvados saw the two dogs directing their angry attention toward one of the thickets in the garden. "Aha," he smiled. "Our noisy midnight visitors tarried too long and have found themselves cornered by the dogs."

He unlocked his weapons case and thrust a rifle into the hands of his coachman and the gardener. He selected a double-barreled shotgun for his own use. "Come," he said, "we'll soon have the miscreants at gunpoint."

After the men had posted themselves at the edge of the garden, the dogs were urged to attack. The two brutes rushed into the thicket with vicious growls. There was a moment of silence, and then the horse canine rumbles of fury turned to plaintive whines and whimpers of terror. The dogs ran out of the thicket with their tails between their legs, and the master could not call them back.

"Well," he chuckled nervously as he cocked both hammers of his shotgun, "whoever is in there can't be that terrible. Come," he urged his servants, "let's find out."

Cautiously, the three men entered the thicket, their firearms cocked and ready. They found nothing—not a footprint, not a shred of clothing on a branch, absolutely nothing. "But, what," the master asked of his men after they had searched in all directions, "could have frightened the dogs so?"

His question was never answered to his satisfaction, but that October midnight had seen the beginning of one of the most prolonged and terrifying of all accounts of poltergeist phenomena. The disturbances which took place in the Norman castle of Calvados from October 12, 1875 to January 30, 1876 were written up and published in the *Annales des Sciences Psychiques* in 1893 by M. J. Morice. Although the master of Calvados kept a diary which could later be used as a documentary of the phenomena, he insisted that his family name not be mentioned in connection with the "haunting." He is, therefore, referred to in the narrative only as M. de X. His immediate family consisted of Mme. de X, and their son. The remainder of the household consisted of Abbe Y., tutor to the son, Maurice; Emile, the coachman; Auguste, the gardener; Amelina, the housemaid; and Celina, the cook. As we shall see throughout this book, the poltergeist is no respecter of persons; the greatest devilment took place in the Abbe's room.

On the evening of October 13th, Abbe Y. came down to the drawing room and presented himself to M. and Mme. de X. "My armchair just moved," he insisted. "I distinctly saw it move out of the corner of my eye."

If the strange incident of the watchdogs had not been so fresh in his mind, M. de X may have accused his son's tutor of too much after-dinner sherry. He calmed the Abbe and returned with him to his room. He attached gummed paper to the foot of the cleric's armchair and fixed it to the floor. "Call me if anything further should occur," M. de X. told the Abbe.

At about ten that evening, the master of Calvados was awakened by the ringing of the Abbe's bell. He got out of bed, hurried to the man's room.

"The whole room has been moving about," the turor whispered from his bed. He had pulled the covers up to the bridge of his nose and peeked out at his employer as if he were a frightened child.

M. de X. saw that the armchair had indeed moved

about a yard and that several candlesticks and statu-
ettes had been upset.

"And there have been rappings on my wall," the Abbe
complained in a voice that quavered on the brink of
hysteria.

M. de X. heard a door open behind him and turned
to see Amelina peeping out from her room across the
hall. Her face was pale. "That's right, sir," she said. "I
heard the rappings, too."

The next evening, the manifestations did not confine
themselves to the Abbe's room. Loud blows were heard
all over. the castle. M. de X. armed his servants and
conducted a search of the entire building. They could
find nothing.

It would be a pattern that they would repeat again
and again as the poltergeist began its seige in earnest.
Night after night, its hammering fist would pound on
doors and rap on walls. The inhabitants of Calvados
castle would not know a night of unmolested slumber
for more than three months.

The curate of the parish arrived to witness the phenomena and was not disappointed. Neither was Marcel
de X., who had come to try to determine the origin of
the manifestations. That night, the sound of a heavy
ball was heard descending the stairs from the second
floor to the first, jumping from step to step.

The parish priest was also invited to stay a night in
the castle. He heard the heavy tread of a giant descending the stairs and proclaimed the activity to be supernatural. Marcel de X. agreed with the priest. He had
quickly concluded that this ghost would be a most
difficult one to "lay" and had decided to leave Calvados
castle to the noisy spirit. He wished M. de X. the best
of luck and returned to his home.

On Halloween, the poltergeist seemed to outdo itself
with a display of prowess that kept the household from
going to bed until three o'clock in the morning.

The center of the activity had now become the green
room, and the phenomena seemed always to either begin or end with loud rappings in this empty room. The
poltergeist now seemed to walk with a tread that "had
nothing human about it. It was like two legs deprived
of their feet and walking on the stumps."

It was during a violent November rainstorm that the poltergeist acquired a voice. High above the howl of the wind and the rumble of the thunder, the beleaguered household heard a long shriek.

"It's a woman!" Amelina, the housemaid, said. "It's a woman outside in the storm calling for help."

Again the cry sounded and everybody looked curiously at one another. "It certainly sounds like a woman," Mme. de X. agreed. "Look out the window and see if someone is outside," she told Celina, the cook.

Celina had just reached the window when the next cry sounded from within the castle. The members of the household gathered together as if seeking strength from their unity. "The doors are all bolted," the Abbe said softly. "I saw to it myself."

Three sorrowful moans sounded as the thing ascended the staircase. The men of Calvados left the sitting room to carefully inspect the castle. They found nothing. There was no woman in the castle, and no sign that anything had entered the castle from the storm. They heard no more sounds until everyone was awakened at 11:45 the next night by terrible sobs and cries coming from the green room. They seemed to be the sounds of a woman in horrible suffering.

During the next few nights, the activity seemed to become intensified and the cries of the sorrowful woman in the green room had become "shrill, furious, despairing cries, the cries of demons or the damned."

Shortly after the "weeping woman" had arrived to add to the confusion at Calvados, a cousin of Mme. de X., an army officer, appeared to pay them a visit. He scoffed at the wild stories the members of the household told him, and against all their pleas, he insisted upon sleeping in the green room.

"I have my revolver always at my side," he told them. "If anything disturbs my sleep, it'll get a bullet in its hide!"

The officer strode boldly to the green room, left a candle burning as a night light, and went straight to sleep. He was awakened a short time later by what seemed to be the soft rustling of a silken robe. He was instantly aware that the candle had been extinguished and that something was tugging at the covers on his bed.

"Who's there?" he demanded gruffly, lighting the candle at his bedside. The candle had no sooner flickered into flame when something extinguished it. Three times he lighted it, and three times he felt a cold breath of air blow it out. The rustling noise seemed to become louder, and something was definitely determined to rob him of his bedclothes.

"Declare yourself or I shall shoot!" he warned, cocking his revolver. The only answer to his demand was an exceptionally violent tug on the covers. He decided to shoot. It was a simple matter to determine where his silent adversary stood by the sound of the rustling and the pull on the bedclothes. The lead slugs of course, struck nothing but the wall, and he dug them out with a knife that next morning. For some reason, however, the poltergeist did leave his covers alone for the rest of the night.

The Abbe continued to fare the worst of any member of the household throughout the duration of the phenomena. No other room in the castle had to entertain such mobile furniture. Whenever the cleric left his room, he always made certain that the windows were bolted and his door was locked. The key to his room was secured to a leather thong which he kept belted to his waist. These precautions never accomplished the slightest bit of good. Upon returning to his room, the Abbe would inevitably find his couch overturned, the cushions scattered about, his windows opened, and his armchair placed on his desk. Once he tried nailing his windows closed. He returned to find the windows wide open, and by way of punishment, the couch cushions were balanced precariously on the outside window sill. Such pranks the Abbe could bear with much more patience than the time the poltergeist dumped every one of his books on the floor. Only the Holy Scriptures remained on the shelves.

The most vicious attack on the clergyman occured once when he knelt at his fireplace stirring the coals, preparatory to placing new kindling on the andirons. Without warning, a huge deluge of water rushed down the chimney, extinguishing the fire, blinding the Abbe with flying sparks, and covering him with ashes.

19

The tutor woefully concluded that such actions could only be the work of his satanic majesty, the Devil.

The only other person who actually suffered physical pain dealt out by the poltergeist was Mme. de X. She was in the act of unlocking a door when the key suddenly disengaged itself from her grip and struck her across the back of her left hand with such force that she bore a large bruise for several days.

One night the invisible creature roamed the corridors as if it were a lonely wayfarer seeking admittance to the rooms of each of the members of the household. It knocked once or twice on the doors of several bedrooms, then, true to pattern, it paused to deal forty consecutive blows to the Abbe's door before it returned to thump about in the green room.

A priest from a neighboring parish heard the distinctive sounds of an animal rubbing itself along the walls when he ventured to stay the night in Calvados castle. Another visitor once witnessed an evening of especially prolonged walking on the part of the poltergeist. "The steps were quite unlike human steps," he later wrote. "No animal could walk like that; it was more like a stick jumping on one of its ends."

The weary household had its only respite during the long seige when the Reverend Father H. L., a Premonstrant Canon, was sent there by the Bishop. From the moment the Reverend Father entered the castle until the moment he left, there was not the slightest sound from the noisy nuisance. But after the clergyman had made his departure, ". . . there was a noise as of a body falling in the first-floor passage, followed by that of a rolling ball giving a violent blow on the door of the green room . . ." and the poltergeist had once again begun his devilment in earnest.

On January 20, 1876, M. de X. left for a two-day visit to his brother, leaving his wife to keep up the journal. Mme. de X. records an eerie bellowing, like that of a bull, which bothered everyone during the master's absence. A weird drumming sound was also introduced during M. de X.'s absence, and a sound "something like strokes with a wand on the stairs."

Upon the master's return to Calvados, the poltergeist became more violent than it had ever been before. It stormed into the rooms of Auguste and Emile and turned their beds over. It whirled into the master's study and heaped books, maps, and papers on the floor. The midnight screams increased in shrillness and urgency and were joined by the roaring of a bull and the furious cries of animals. A rhythmic tapping paraded up and down the corridors as if a small drum and bugle corps were conducting manuevers. The rappings seemed to direct themselves, for the first time, to the door of Maurice, the son of M. and Mme. de X. Terrible screams sounded outside his room, and the violence of the successive blows on his door shook every window on the floor.

On the night of January 26th, the parish priest arrived with the intention of conducting the rites of exorcism. He had also arranged for a Novena of Masses to be said at Lourdes which would coincide with his performance of the ancient ritual of "putting a spirit to rest."

The priest's arrival was greeted by a long, drawn-out cry and what sounded like a stampede of hoofed creatures running from the first floor passage. There came a noise similar to that of heavy boxes being moved, and the door to Maurice's room began to shake as if something demanded entrance. The last days of the poltergeist are significant in that a great deal of the activity began to center around the adolescent son. It was though the psychic tremors of puberty had somehow set the manifestations in motion or had reactivated unseen forces that had lain dormant in the old castle.

The rites of exorcism reached their climax at 11:15 on the night of January 29th. From the stairway came a piercing cry, like that of a beast that had been dealt its deathblow. A flurry of rappings began to rain on the door of the green room. At 12:55, the startled inhabitants of Calvados castle heard the voice of a man in the first-floor passage. "It seemed to cry twice Ha! Ha!" M. de X. records in his journal. "Immediately there were ten resounding blows, shaking everything all around. One blow on the door of the green room. Then the sound of coughing in the first-floor passage."

The "sound of coughing" may very well have been the poltergeist's death-rattle. The family rose and cautiously began to move about the castle. The priest slumped in exhaustion, sweat beading his forehead from the long ordeal. There was no sound of the hammering fist, no raucous screams, no shaking of doors, no shifting of furniture. They found a large earthenware plate which had been broken into ten pieces at the door to Mme. de X.'s room. No one had ever seen the plate before that night.

"Everything has stopped," M. de X. wrote in his journal.

His elation was somewhat premature. Several days after the exorcisms had been performed, Mme. de X. was sitting at a writing desk when an immense packet of holy medals and crosses dropped in front of her on her paper. It was as if the poltergeist had suffered a momentary set-back and was announcing that it must retreat for a time to recuperate and lick its wounds.

Towards the end of August, soft knockings and rappings began to be heard. On the third Sunday in September, the drawing-room furniture was arranged in horseshoe fashion with the couch in the middle.

"The Devil has held council and is about to begin again," a parish priest was heard to moan.

A few days afterward, Mme. de X. lay terrified in her bed and watched the latch to her room unbolt itself. M. de X. was out of the castle for a few days on business, and she was alone with the servants.

The duration of the phenomena was much briefer this time, and the poltergeist seemed to be content to play the organ and to move an occasional bit of furniture about the room of Maurice's new tutor. Eventually the phenomena became weaker and weaker until the only thing that haunted Calvados castle was the memory of those terrible months when a poltergeist ran rampant in its corridors.

SATAN AND THE FARMER'S DAUGHTERS

"MERCY UPON US," Mrs. Rebecca Jane Sybert said to her son Frank, "your Bertha's bouncin' around in her bed again."

"Bertha!" the rugged mountaineer yelled at his nine-year-old daughter. "You stop that bouncin', you hear?

22

You're going to fall outa bed just like you did last night."

"I can't help it, Pa," Bertha said, her voice quavering on the verge of tears. "It's the spirit that's doin' it."

"Mind your tongue, child," her grandmother scolded. "Don't talk of such foolishness."

"Settle down in there, or I'll be takin' a switch to you," her father promised in a harsh voice.

Frank Sybert narrowed his eyes in frustrated paternal wrath as the squeaking of the old bed in his daughter's room began to increase in its intensity. He clomped his heavy boots down on the rough planking of their mountain home and rose to his feet with determination.

"Don't be too hard on the child, Frank," Rebecca Jane cautioned. "She misses her mother."

Frank Sybert nodded. "But she has to learn to mind." He walked to the door of his daughter's room, cleared his throat preparatory to delivering a stern lecture. His brain struggled with the right combination of words that would tread the thin line between fatherly firmness and understanding. Whatever tact he had decided upon, his lecture was never delivered. He stood with unbelieving eyes as he watched the foot of his daughter's bed raise itself three feet into the air, then drop to the floor with a sudden crash.

"It's the spirit, Pa," Bertha sobbed. "He's followed me to bed again."

Frank Sybert knelt to look under the bed. If some prankster had hidden himself under the bed, he would really give him "what-for!" There was no one there. And the bed was raising again, the foot lifting itself higher and higher. The mountaineer threw himself on the bed to lower it, but the "spirit" didn't seem to mind the extra passenger at all. The foot of the bed hung suspended with Frank Sybert peering cautiously over the edge, trying desperately to "figure out the trick."

For more than forty nights, the "spirit" followed young Bertha Sybert to bed, and scores of the curious came to Wallins Creek near St. Charles, Virginia to witness the animated bed.

One night two hefty farmers joined Frank Sybert in an attempt to hold the bed down, but the Herculean poltergeist lifted them with ease.

In time, Bertha began to speak to her spirit, and by

23

saying "sake-sake big," she could make the bed bounce violently.

But the ordeal in that winter of 1938 soon began to take its physical toll on the child. She became covered with bruises and "sore all over" from the nocturnal pranks of the spirit, which would not allow her to sleep. At the end of a month, she was in such a weakened condition that a physician advised hospitalization.

"I wish he would leave me alone now," the girl told a United Press reporter, who had come to talk with "Bouncing Bertha."

"If there is such a thing as witchery," Frank Sybert said to the reporter, "I sincerely believe that my daughter is bewitched. It couldn't be a ghost. It must be a witch because we've made every known investigation to determine its cause."

If one of the devil's handmaidens received the blame for the phenomena at Willins Creek, his satanic majesty was personally accredited with the disturbances that came to a climax in Iowa in September, 1928. From her fourteenth year to her fortieth, a woman had sustained manifestations after she had been "cursed by her father." During a marathon ritual of exorcism, which lasted twenty-three days, the Reverend Celestine Kapsner of St. John's Abbey, Collegeville, Minnesota managed, at last, to put the extraordinary poltergeist to rest.

One could theorize that the long duration of the phenomena was due to the intense psychological reaction that a devoutly religious girl would under-go after she had been "cursed by her father" and that this psychic shock, combined with the trauma of sexual change, had produced the "bundle of projected repressions" that specialized in levitation activity. But Reverend Kapsner attributed the disturbances to diabolical possession—specifically, the devils Beelzebub, Lucifer, Judas, Jacob, and Mina. The Reverend Father wrote an account of the exhaustive exorcism in 1935 in a pamphlet entitled, *Begone Satan!*

The pamphlet can hardly be judged on its literary merits, but it does present a fascinating account of a dramatic poltergeist case. One can imagine the effect the phenomena had on the Father and the nuns who attended him when one reads of the woman's ability to

24

fly up to the ceiling and to stick to it "with cat-like grips." A floating parishioner would be disconcerting to the most liberal clergyman.

In one instance, the narrative tells of the nuns binding the woman securely to an iron bed so that she might remain stationary during the ceremony of exorcism. In addition to the bonds, the nuns rested the weight of their own bodies across the torso of the afflicted woman. All these precautions were useless: "Hardly had the Father begun the formula of exorcism . . . when a terrible scene followed. With lightning speed the possessed dislodged herself from her bed and the hands of her protectors; her body was carried through the air, landed high above the door of the room, and clung to the wall . . . All present were struck with a trembling fear. Father alone kept his peace: 'Pull her down. She must be brought back to her place upon the bed!'

"Real force had to be applied to her feet to bring her down from the high position on the wall. The mystery was that she could have clung to the wall at all!"

THE POLTERGEIST THAT KILLED

It should be obvious by now that the conception of the poltergeist as being simply a fun-loving prankster is an erroneous one. The intelligence that directs the phenomena is motivated more often by malice than by mischief. Although physical violence toward a certain member of the family is characteristic of several poltergeist cases, there is only one recorded instance where the poltergeist was actually responsible for murder. On December 19, 1820, John Bell was poisoned by the "witch" that had inhabited their home for four years.

The disturbances began with mysterious rappings on the windows of the Bell's cabin near Clarksville, Tennessee. Elizabeth Bell began to complain of an invisible "rat" gnawing on her bedpost at night. The entire family experienced the midnight confusion of having their covers pulled off their beds. Everyone heard a strange sucking noise, an eerie smacking of lips, as if an invisible baby were being nursed.

Several investigators of poltergeist phenomena have

noted these same peculiar sounds of psychic "nursing." Some researchers have noted that these "signal" noises often occur shortly before an evening of particularly violent disturbances. It is as if the poltergeist is some kind of obscene infant being "born" of projected frustrations and repressions. Sacheverell Sitwell wrote of the "birth" of a poltergeist in this manner: "It babbles, as though in the struggles of life or death. It is dying, or but just born, an embryonic phantasm which is only upon the borderlands, upon one frontier or the other, of human life. None can pity it or feel sorrow for it. There is an obscene or drivelling sense to it . . . It is in all things unholy, unhallowed, and not human. Who can doubt that it is the projection, not of the brain, but of the obscene senses, of the deep, hidden underworld which is at the back of every mind."

When the Bell family arose one morning, stones littered the floor of their front room and the furniture had been overturned. The children, Elizabeth, John, Drewry, Joel, and Richard were goggle-eyed and spoke of ghosts and goblins. John Bell lectured his family severely: "We shall keep this problem to ourselves. We don't want our family to become the subject for common and unsavory gossip."

That night, Richard was awakened by something pulling his hair, raising his head right off the pillow. Joel began screaming at his brother's plight, and from her room, Elizabeth began howling that the gnawing rat had begun to pull her hair, too.

Most of the family awakened the next day with sore scalps, and John reversed his decision. It was obvious that the Bell family needed help. That day he would confide in James Johnson, their nearest neighbor and closest friend.

Johnson accompanied his friend to the cabin that evening. The tale that Bell told was an incredible one, but Johnson knew that his neighbor was not given to flights of fancy. While he watched at Elizabeth's bedside that night, Johnson saw the young girl receive several blows on the cheeks from an invisible antagonist.

"Stop in the name of the Lord Jesus Christ!" Johnson adjured the phantom assailant.

There was no activity from the poltergeist for several

minutes, then Betsy's hair received a yank that brought a cry of pain from her lips. Again Johnson adjured the "evil spirit" and it released the girl's hair.

"I conclude that the spirit understands the human language," Johnson told Bell. The wise Mr. Johnson was also able to determine that Betsy was the center of the haunting. He met with other neighbors, and they decided to help the Bell family as best they could. First a committee decided to keep watch at the Bell house all night to try to placate the spirit. All this act accomplished was to bring about an especially vicious attack on the unfortunate Betsy. A number of neighbors volunteered their own daughters to sleep with the girl, but this only managed to terrorize the other girls as well. Nor did it accomplish any useful purpose to take Betsy out of the cabin into the home of neighbors—the trouble simply followed her there and upset the entire house.

By now the haunting had achieved wide notoriety, and the disturbances were thought to be the work of a witch, who had set her evil spirits upon the Bell family. Each night the house was filled with those who sat up trying to get the "witch" to talk or to communicate with them by rapping on the walls or by smacking its lips. There seems little doubt that somehow the phenomena was able to "feed" itself upon the psyches of these "true believers." The disturbances soon became powerful enough to venture outside the cabin and away from Betsy, its center of energy. Neighbors reported seeing lights "like candles or lamps" flitting through the fields, and farmers began to suffer stone-throwing attacks from the Bell Witch.

These particular peltings seemed to have been more in the nature of fun than some of the other manifestations of the poltergeist. Young boys in the area would often play catch with the Witch if she happened to throw something at them on their way home from school. Once an observer witnessed several boys get suddenly pelted with sticks that flew from a nearby thicket. The sticks did not strike the boys with much force, and, with a great deal of laughter, the boys scooped the sticks up and hurled them back into the thicket. Once again, the sticks came flying back out. The observer cut notches in several of the sticks with

27

his knife before the boys once again returned the Witch's volley. He was able to identify his markings when the playful poltergeist once again flung the sticks from the thicket.

The Witch was not so gentle with the scoffers who had come to the Bell home to "expose the manifestations as trickery." Those who stayed the night invariably had their covers jerked from their beds. If they resisted the Witch's yanking, they were slapped soundly on the face. "The blows were heard distinctly," one of the Bell family noted in a diary, "like the open palm of a heavy hand. . . ."

Spiritists, clergymen, reporters, and curiosity seekers had waged a ceaseless campaign that sought to urge the Witch to talk and declare herself and her intentions. At last their efforts were rewarded. At first the voice was only a whistling kind of indistinct babble, then it became bolder—a husky whisper speaking from darkened corners. At last, it became a full-toned voice that spoke not only in darkness but also in lighted rooms and, finally, during the day as well as the night.

Immediately the charge of ventriloquism was heard from the skeptical. To put a halt to the accusations of trickery, John Jr. brought in a doctor, who placed his hand over Betsy's mouth and listened at her throat while the Witch's voice chatted amicably from a far corner of the room. The doctor decreed that the girl was "in no way connected with these sounds." A modern day psychical researcher would have qualified that statement by adding "at least not by ventriloquism." Twelve-year-old Betsy Bell had begun to suffer from seizures and fainting spells very similar to those which mediums undergo before entering into trance. Observers noted that the spells came on at regular hours, just before the Witch put in an appearance. After Betsy recovered, the Witch would begin to speak. The Witch was always silent while the girl lay prostrate upon her bed.

From the very beginning of the Witch's visitation, it had minced no words in its dislike of John Bell, Betsy's father. "I'll keep after him until the end of his days!" the Witch often swore to visitors in the Bell home. "Old Jack Bell's days are numbered."

Even before the Witch had begun to manifest itself

by the rapping on the windows and the hair-pulling, John Bell had complained of a strange pain in his throat. He described it as feeling like "a stick stuck crosswise, punching each side of my jaws." As the phenomena progressed, Bell was often plagued by a tongue that swelled against his mouth, so that "he could neither talk nor eat for ten or fifteen hours."

It has been suggested that the on-set of John Bell's physical afflictions and his daughter's psychic persecution was no coincidence. Dr. Nandor Fodor, writing of the Bell Witch, makes the observation that the swelling of Bell's tongue suggests that he may have been keeping a dreadful secret that sought physical release. Dr. Fodor also speculates that Betsy, approaching puberty, may have undergone a shocking sexual experience for which her father was responsible. "It was probably to save her reason," Dr. Fodor wrote, "that a fragment of her mind was split off and became the Bell Witch." If this theory is true, it may account for the remarkable range and power of the Bell poltergeist. Psychically, the phenomena was being fed by sexual shock, pubertal change, and a father's guilt.

To a visitor's question concerning its identity, the Witch once answered: "I am a spirit who was once very happy, but who has been disturbed and made unhappy. I will remain in this house and worry old Jack Bell until I kill him."

Later, the Witch declared itself to be the spirit of an Indian and sent the family on a wild "bone chase" to gather up all of its skeletal remains. "If my bones are all put back together, I'll be able to rest in peace," the poltergeist lied to them.

"I'm really the ghost of old Kate Batts," the Witch told the family with a merry cackle as they confessed their inability to find all of the Indian's bones. Kate Batts had been an eccentric recluse who had earned the appellation of "witch" from the citizens of Clarksville. When the word spread that it was the ghost of old Kate who was haunting the Bells, the entire mystery became much more believable to several doubting neighbors.

The Bell home became crowded, indeed, when the Witch's "family" moved in with her. Four hell-raisers named Blackdog, Mathematics, Cypocryphy, and Jerusalem, each speaking in distinct voices of their own, made every night a party night during their stay with their "mother." The sounds of raucous laughter rattled the shingles of the Bell home, and witnesses noted the strong scent of whiskey that permeated every room in the house.

When two local preachers arrived to investigate the disturbances, the Witch delivered each of their Sunday sermons word for word and in a perfect imitation of their own voices.

The Bell Witch was, as are all poltergeists, adept at producing odd objects apparently from thin air. Once, at one of Mrs. Bell's Bible study groups, the ladies were showered with fresh fruits. Betsy's friends were treated to bananas at one of her birthday parties. "Those came from the West Indies," the Witch told the delighted girls. "I picked them myself."

Although the father, John Bell, was the butt of malicious pranks and cruel blows, Mrs. Bell was looked after solicitously by the Witch. Once when Mrs. Bell was ill, the Witch was heard to say: "Poor Luce. Hold out your hands, I have something for you."

Mrs. Bell held out her hands and a large quantity of hazelnuts dropped into her palms. "Eat them," the Witch instructed her. "They will do you good."

"But I cannot crack them," Mrs. Bell said weakly.

"Then I shall do it for you," the Witch answered. Family and neighbors watched in wide-eyed fascination as the nuts cracked open and the meats were sorted from the shells.

Next to the materialization of fruits and nuts, the Witch was especially fond of producing pins and needles. Mrs. Bell was provided with enough pins to supply the entire county, but sometimes the Witch would impishly hide them in the bedclothes or in chair cushions—points out.

John Jr., Betsy's favorite brother, was the only member of the family besides the mother who received decent treatment from the Witch. Joel and Richard were often whipped soundly by the invisible force, and Drewry was so frightened of the Witch that he never married, fearing that the entity might someday return and single out his own family for particular attention. John Jr.

was the only one of Betsy's brothers who could "sass back" at the Witch and get away with it. The Witch even went to special pains to get John Jr. to like it, and the mysterious entity often performed demonstrations of ability solely for his benefit.

Elizabeth and her father, of course, received the brunt of the Witch's ill nature. The cruelest act perpetrated on Betsy was the breaking of her engagement to Joshua Gardner. The two young people were acclaimed by friends to be "ideally suited for one another," but the Witch protested violently when the engagement was announced.

"She will never know a day of happiness if she marries Joshua," the Witch told John Jr. "You must aid me in preventing the union."

The Witch screamed at Joshua whenever he entered the Bell home and embarrassed both young people by shouting obscenities about them in front of their friends. Richard Bell noted in his diary that the "vile devil . . . never ceased to practice upon her fears, insult her modesty, stick pins in her body, pinching and bruising her flesh, slapping her cheeks, dishevelling and tangling her hair, tormenting her in many ways until she surrendered that most cherished hope which animates every young heart."

A friend of the family, Frank Miles, learned of the Witch's objection to Betsy's engagement and resolved to stand up to the "evil spirit" on her behalf.

As an elderly woman in her eighties, Elizabeth still remembered how Miles "fairly shook the house, stamping on the floor, swearing terribly."

"Take any form you so desire," Miles threatened, "and I'll take you on." He made motions in the air as if warming up for a wrestling match. "Just let me get a hold of you, and we'll soon send you packing. I'm not afraid of an invisible windbag."

Suddenly Miles' head jerked backwards as if a solid slap had stung his cheeks. He put up his forearms to block a series of facial blows, then dropped his guard as he received a vicious punch in the stomach. Miles slumped against a wall, desperately shaking his head to recover his senses.

31

"Begone," he heard the Witch's voice warn him, "or I'll knock your block off!"

Frank Miles looked helplessly at Betsy Bell, who had watched the one-sided boxing match. Reluctantly, he picked up his hat and coat. A man couldn't fight an enemy he couldn't see.

With the decisive defeat of her champion, Betsy had no choice but to give in to the Witch's demands and break her engagement with Joshua Gardner. On the night in which Betsy returned the ring, the Witch's laughter could be heard ringing victoriously from every room in the house.

Shortly after the entity had accomplished the severing of Betsy's marriage agreement with her fiancee, it once more began to concentrate its energy on the destruction of John Bell. Richard was walking with his father on that day in December of 1920 when John Bell collapsed into a spasmodically convulsing heap. Young Richard was terrified by the agonies that beset his wretched father and wrote later that his facial contortions were so hideous that they seemed to "convert him into a very demon to swallow me up."

John Bell was brought home to his bed where he lay for several days in a very weakened condition. Even during the man's illness, the Witch would not leave him in peace, but continued to torment him by slapping his face and throwing his legs into the air. On the morning of December 19, 1820, John Bell lapsed into a stupor from which he would never be aroused. John Jr. went quickly to the medicine cabinet to obtain his father's prescription and found instead "a smoky looking vial, which was about one-third full of dark colored liquid."

"It's no use to try to revive Old Jack," the Witch cackled. "I've got him at last."

"Where did this vial come from!" John Jr. demanded of the voice.

"I put it there last night," the Witch answered smugly. "I gave Old Jack a big dose of it while he was asleep. I fixed him!"

John Jr. sent for the doctor. When the physician arrived, he asked one of the boys to fetch a cat from the barn. While John Jr. held the cat, the doctor dipped a straw into the dark vial and wiped it on the animal's

32

tongue. The cat jumped into the air, whirled about on the floor, and "died very quick."

The Witch sang bawdy songs all during John Bell's funeral and annoyed the assembled mourners with the sounds of its crude celebration throughout the man's last rites.

After the death of her father, the Witch behaved much better toward Betsy. It never again inflicted pain upon her and actually addressed her in terms of endearment. The psychic energy which nurtured the poltergeist seemed to be waning. During the rest of the winter and on into the spring months, the manifestations decreased steadily. Then, one night after the evening meal, a large smoke ball seemed to roll down from the chimney of the fireplace out into the room. As it burst, a voice told the family: "I'm going now, and I will be gone for seven years."

True to its word, the Witch returned to the homestead in 1828. Betsy had entered into a successful marriage with another man; John Jr. had married and now farmed land of his own. Only Mrs. Bell, Joel, and Richard remained on the home place. The disturbances consisted of the Witch's most elementary pranks—rappings, scratchings, pulling the covers off the bed—and the family agreed to ignore the unwanted guest. Their psychology worked, and the Witch left them after two weeks of pestering them for attention. The entity sought out John Jr. and told him in a fit of pique that it would return to one of his descendants in "one hundred years and seven."

Dr. Charles Bailey Bell should have been the recipient of the Bell Witch's unwelcome return visit, but Dr. Bell and his family survived the year 1935 without hearing the slightest unexplained scratch or undetermined rapping. Dr. Bell has written the official record of the mysterious disturbances endured by his ancestors in *The Bell Witch. A Mysterious Spirit.*

Dr. Bell notes the precognitive powers of the Witch in a series of "wonderful things" and prophecies which the entity revealed to his grandfather, John Bell, Jr. The Witch predicted the Civil War, the emancipation of the Negroes, the acceleration of the United States as a world power, the two world wars (the date for

World War II was off by only four years), and the destruction of our civilization by "rapidly expanding heat, followed by a mighty explosion." Thankfully, this last prediction is not dated.

THE BUG-EYED MONSTER'S INVISIBLE FANGS

THE EIGHTEEN-YEAR-OLD girl writhed on the floor of the jail cell and moaned as if in terrible pain. She sat upright, her eyes wide, her arms flailing at an invisible foe. "Here he comes again!" she screamed. "The monster has come again to bite me!"

The policeman, who had been posted to observe the girl, chuckled at the distraught young woman's hysterical screams. He did not believe her wild tale of some bug-eyed monster with a black cape that flew around trying to chew her up. When the police had found her, she had been twitching about on the streets of Manila, sobbing for someone to protect her from the monster. Her strange behavior had attracted a small crowd of observers from a nearby tavern, who had stood by cheering her on, enjoying her demonstration immensely. She had been taken into custody under the suspicion of being either a drug addict or a young woman who had become indiscreet with a bottle of alcohol.

"Don't worry," the policeman told teen-aged Clarita Villaneuva as she crouched in terror behind the bunk in her cell. "No monster can get you in there. He couldn't get through the bars."

"But he is coming!" Clarita shrieked. "And he is drifting right through the bars!"

Then, before the officer's startled eyes, livid teeth marks appeared on Clarita's upper arms and shoulders. He quickly opened the cell door, knelt beside the girl and helped her to her feet. Again the girl screamed and more red welts appeared on her arm. It was as if an invisible monster had wrapped its entire mouth around her slim arm and had sunk its teeth deep into her flesh. The officer helped Clarita into the hall and together they fled the cell to seek out his captain. The captain took one look at the two of them and phoned the Mayor as well as the Chief of Police and the Medical Examiner.

The Mayor and the police official had already completed their bewildered examination of Clarita when the doctor arrived, muttering his disapproval at being dragged out of bed in the middle of the night to observe a young woman who was obviously suffering from epileptic seizures and was inflicting wounds upon herself.

"Self-inflicted?" the Chief frowned at the medical examiner. "How does one bite himself on the back of his neck?"

Gently, Mayor Arsenio Lacson questioned Clarita while the doctor examined her. What, he wanted to know, was attacking her?

The girl sobbed that she certainly did not know its name. It resembled a man with a long, flowing black cape. It was very ugly and came at her with its fangs bared and ready to sink into her flesh.

The medical examiner traced a forefinger over the indentations in the girl's skin. They certainly appeared to be the prints of teeth, he had to admit. And, he went on, the girl was not drunk, nor was she under the influence of any drug.

The Police Chief noted the date, May 10, 1951, on the calendar. A religious man, he had briefly entertained the notion that this may be the onset of a manifestation of stigmata, but there were no special holy days in the Philippines during the month of May.

Clarita spent the rest of the night on a bench in the front office of the police station, closely attended by an officer, who had been assigned the eerie task of "keeping watch for the monster."

The next morning, the girl was brought to court to face the charges of vagrancy that had been levied against her. There, before the incredulous eyes of the entire court, Clarita endured another attack by her invisible monster. Reporters rushed to stand beside her for a closer look. Dr. Mariana Lara, the Medical Examiner, took the girl in his arms as she swooned from the excruciating pain of unseen jaws that attached themselves to her flesh.

"This girl is definitely not having an epileptic fit," Dr. Lara told the reporters. "These teeth prints are real, but they are most certainly not self-inflicted."

There was no need to attest to the reality of the teeth

marks to the reporters. They were serving as startled witnesses to the cruel indentations that were appearing on the girl's arms, shoulders, palms, and neck.

Dr. Lara told a police officer to send at once for the Mayor—and the Archbishop. "This is outside my realm of physiology and medicine," he said. "Perhaps a clergyman will be of more value in this case than a doctor."

By the time Mayor Lacson arrived, the unfortunate girl had become a veritable mass of deeply embedded teeth prints and swollen and bruised flesh.

"You poor girl," the Mayor commiserated, taking one of her hands into his own. Then, while he held Clarita's hand, deep teeth marks appeared on opposite sides of her index finger, as if a hungry fiend were trying to chew the digit off.

The Mayor ordered the girl into his car. "We must take her to a hospital!"

Dr. Lara agreed, and the two men helped Clarita into the Mayor's car. The driver thought that Clarita was a victim of some horrible beating until the teeth began to attack her in the automobile.

"Quickly driver," Mayor Lacson ordered. "We must get this girl to a hospital."

The driver did not need to be told twice. Beads of sweat coursed freely down his cheeks as he wheeled the Mayor's car through the Manila traffic, one eye on the signals and the other on the tortured girl who sat between him and the doctor.

For some reason, the attacks ceased when the girl entered the hospital, and she began to recover the health that had been deteriorated by the "monster's" merciless jaws. Clarita Villaneuva never again suffered from the terrible invisible teeth that tore at her flesh.

"This whole phenomena simply defies rational explanation," Dr. Lara once commented. "I don't mind saying that I was scared out of my wits."

Such violent manifestations as the inflicting of bites and scratches is, although quite rare, not unknown in poltergeist disturbances. For whatever reason, that fragment of mind, which has managed to free itself and to exist independently of the original personality, seems to delight in dealing out physical torment to its energy center. As we have seen, it is almost always the "feeder"

36

of the poltergeist's energy who has to endure the brunt of the phenomena. Most often this takes the form of rappings on the bedstead, or some such relatively gentle activity, and is punctuated only occasionally by the pulling of the hair or by a slap in the face. In some instances, however, whether it be charged by feelings of guilt and the need for punishment or by the desire to call attention to the original personality in an extreme and dramatic manner, the poltergeist can attain terrible teeth and cruel claws that can inflict vicious wounds upon the unconscious generator of the phenomena.

JEF THE MAGIC MONGOOSE

IT WAS in the fall of 1931 that the mysterious talking animal came to live with the James T. Irving family on the Isle of Man.

His daughter, Voirrey, saw it first, just seconds before Mr. Irving himself caught a glimpse of it. It was as large as a full-grown rat with a flat snout and a small yellow face.

"Maybe that's what was making that scratching noise in the parlor last night," Voirrey suggested.

The strange beast would not long be satisfied with such simple effects as scratching the beams that partitioned the rooms of the Irving home. It began to mimic the calls and cries of barnyard animals and poultry. Mr. Irving then made a marvelous discovery—the rodent-like creature was extraordinarily intelligent. Members of the family had but to call out the name of an animal or bird and the mysterious creature would respond with the correct imitation.

The night noises began to increase, and the family was beginning to find them less than pleasant. The animal would blow, spit, and growl about the dark corners of the bedrooms, keeping the family awake until all hours of the night. Once, in an effort to lull herself to sleep, Voirrey began to chant nursery rhymes aloud. She was startled to hear the weird animal begin to repeat the rhymes after she had finished. In an excited voice, she called to her parents to come and share her discovery. The creature could now talk. Mr. and Mrs.

Irving stood at the door of the daughter's bedroom and exchanged incredulous stares. The animal's voice, although a full two octaves higher than any human's, was clear and distinct as it sing-songed nursery rhymes.

The animal quickly put itself on an intimate basis with the Irvings. It called Mr. Irving "Jim" and his wife, "Maggie." It carried on long conversations with them and announced that it had chosen to make its home with them. The latter bit of news was received by the Irvings with a marked lack of enthusiasm. The family was able to get so little sleep that Mr. Irving was almost to the point of selling the farm and leaving. He realized, however, that it would not be easy to sell a farm that was not only quite isolated but now seemed to have acquired a "haunt." And their talking rodent was no longer a secret. On January 10, 1932, the Manchester *Daily Dispatch* and the London *Daily Sketch* ran articles on the mysterious "talking weasel."

"Have I ever heard a weasel speak?" asked a reporter for the *Daily Dispatch*. "I do not know, but I do know that I heard, today, a voice I never imagined could issue from a human throat."

The journalist found the Irving family "sane, honest, and responsible folk not likely to indulge in difficult long-drawn-out practical jokes to make them the talk of the world."

James Irving kept insisting to visiting newspapermen that "there are no spooks here! The farm is not haunted. All that has happened is that a strange animal has taken up its abode here."

Since the first night of the animal's arrival, however, the "talking weasel" evidenced some obvious poltergeistic features. Strange scratchings and unexplainable sounds were followed by the equally mysterious and unaccountable moving of furniture and the "tossing" of small objects. The poltergeist's appearance, in this instance, seems not to have been connected with the advent of puberty. Irving's daughter was nearly thirteen at the on-set of the phenomena, and she was long past this stage of her development by the time the disturbances ceased four years later. A noted parapsychologist later suggested that a part of James Irving's splitoff mind may have entered into the animal's mental orbit and stimulated this most unusual form of development. This poltergeist did something which no other entity of its ilk has ever done before or since in that it provided meat for the family table. Over fifty rabbits were left on the kitchen floor by the thoughtful poltergeist. It is interesting to note that each of the rabbits had been strangled. If a true weasel or mongoose had done the stalking, it would surely have used its teeth on the throat of its prey. It is also important to note that James Irving had traveled widely before settling on the Isle of Man. He could speak German, Russian, and a smattering of several Indian dialects. Later on, as the phenomena increased and became strengthened, the strange animal claimed to be a mongoose born near Delhi, India, and it often used Indian words and sang Indian folk songs.

The animal's claim of being a mongoose was reinforced by the fact that a farmer in Doarlish Cashen had once bought a number of the creatures to kill off the rabbits that had become a threat to his field crops. No one ever received more than a glimpse of the animal that had moved in with the Irvings, but those who had seen the strange thing described it in terms that might well have applied to a small mongoose.

James Irving began calling his uninvited guest "Jef." This name met with the approval of the self-proclaimed mongoose. "When I was in India, I lived with a tall man who wore a green turban on his head," Jef informed Irving. "I was born on June 7, 1852."

"But," Irving stammered, "that makes you 79 years old!"

The talkative mongoose laughed and began singing a Hindu folk song.

Jef's activities were by no means confined to the Irving cottage. He wandered far afield to stalk rabbits for the family meal, and he took delight in hiding in village garages and in bringing back gossip to share with the Irvings.

The weird entity also had a cruel streak which it most often indulged on the villagers. Once, it terrorized a group of men repairing a road by carrying off their lunches. Several of the workmen swore that they had seen lunchbags being toted off by some invisible force. Another time, it was blamed for striking a garage mechanic with a large iron bolt. Irving later attested that Jef had boasted of the deed.

Harry Price, the famous psychical researcher and "ghost hunter," sent an associate to the Isle of Man to investigate the truth of the news stories that he had begun to collect on the "haunt" of Cashen's Gap. It was a rare stranger who made a favorable impression on Jef, and Price's investigator, a Captain Macdonald, was no exception to the rule.

"That bloody man is a doubter!" Jef screamed from his hiding place. "Get him out of here!" When Macdonald arrived with a camera and tried to coax Jef out of his crack to pose for a picture, the mongoose displayed its ill humor by squirting water on the investigator. Later, it hurled a needle at the man, which missed him and struck a tea pot.

"He often throws things at us," Irving told the researcher.

Then the mongoose was seen sitting on a wall in the farmyard. "Quickly," Macdonald pleaded with Voirrey, handing her the camera, "see if you can approach it and get a picture of the beast."

The girl began walking towards Jef, speaking to the entity in a low, pleasant voice. She lifted the camera to sight the animal through the lens, but it was gone before she could click the shutter.

Captain Macdonald received little more than the animal's curses for his troubles, but at least he had heard the mysterious mongoose and had got a glimpse of it. When Harry Price came out to the island to investigate the disturbances, the temperamental Jef was silent during the entire duration of his stay.

The poltergeist in animal form demanded to be served food by the Irvings and was especially fond of bananas and pastries. Although it often seemed genuinely concerned about the family's welfare (as witness the providing of freshly killed rabbits for the table), the mongoose did not relish any open expression of affection. Once Mrs. Irving put her hand into Jef's hole and began to stroke the animal's fur. She instantly withdrew her hand with a sharp cry of pain. Jef had bitten her and had drawn blood. "He gripped my hand like a vise," Mrs. Irving said.

The fact that Mrs. Irving had actually touched the manifestation encouraged Harry Price to suggest that the family attempt to obtain a bit of Jef's fur for laboratory analysis. As if it had read their thoughts, the mongoose awakened the family late one night and promised the Irvings that it was going to present them with "something precious." Jef directed them to a particular bowl on a shelf in the kitchen. The eager Irvings turned on the lights and hurried quickly downstairs to seek out the appointed bowl. There, in its center, was a tuft of fur.

James Irving mailed the fur off the next morning to Harry Price, who, in turn, relayed it to the London Zoo. Unfortunately, it turned out that the cunning Jef was simply playing a prank. The fur was that of a dog, not a mongoose.

Determined to obtain some shred of tangible evidence of the creature's physical existence, Price sent the Irvings four plasticine blocks so that Jef might stamp the impressions of his feet in the doughy material. James Irving set the blocks in Jef's hole and coaxed his strange house guest to imprint its feet in the plasticine.

The next morning, the family awakened to Jef's lusty cursing: "It was hard as hell," the mongoose complained. "But I did it. Go'n' look!"

This time it seemed as though the animal had really co-operated with the Irving's desire to secure a permanent memento of its visitation. Excitedly, James Irving shipped the casts off to Harry Price and anxiously went back to his farm to await the results of analysis and identification.

"One print might have been made by a dog," Mr. R. I. Peacock of the British Natural History Museum's Zoological Department concluded. "The others are of no mammal known to me unless it is that of an American raccoon . . . I must add that I do not think these casts represent foot tracks at all. Most certainly none of them were made by a mongoose."

R. S. Lambert, an associate of Harry Price's, suggested that Jef was voice and nothing more, but witnesses claimed to have seen something scampering about that was decidedly a physical being. James Irving wrote in a journal which he kept throughout the duration of the phenomena: "The mongoose said to my wife, 'I know what I am, but I shan't tell you. I might let you see me, but not to get to know me. I'm a freak. I've hands and feet. If you saw me, you'd be petrified, mummified . . . I'm a ghost in form of a weasel."

Jef continued to live with the Irvings for four years, alternately chatting with them or cursing them. Then, the mysterious talking mongoose simply seemed to fade into nothingness and became but another of the Isle of Man's many legends.

In 1947, a farmer actually did shoot a mongoose near Cashen's Gap. There was a great deal of conjecture on the part of the villagers whether or not this animal might have been a descendant of one of the mongooses turned loose in 1914, but the farmer was certain that the creature had not talked to him before he pulled the trigger.

THE POLTERGEIST THAT LOVED TO DANCE

MR. SHCHAPOFF had been away from his large country estate near Orensburg in the province of Uralsk in Russia, but when he returned on November 16, 1870, he found his household in an uproar over a dancing ghost.

According to his wife, their baby daughter had been fussy on the night of the 14th and had not been at all eager to go to sleep. Mrs. Shchapoff asked Maria, the cook, if she would see to the child. Maria entertained the girl with her harmonica while her mistress and the miller's wife gossipped in the living room.

"How good Maria is with children," Mrs. Shchapoff smiled as she heard the sounds of the cook's feet tapping the floor in a brisk three-step dance. "If all else fails, she dances for the child. That always puts the little one to sleep."

The miller's wife was in the act of nodding her head in agreement when she suddenly straightened and opened her mouth in surprise and terror. "Who is that at the window?"

Mrs. Shchapoff turned and saw nothing to cause the woman so much alarm. "Why," she said, "there's no one there."

"I thought I saw a horrid face looking in at us," the miller's wife said. She was visibly shaken and disturbed. "It was probably only a shadow of some sort."

Maria entered the room and told her mistress that the child was now sound asleep. Mrs. Shchapoff thanked the cook and dismissed her for the evening. Maria stifled a yawn and announced that she, too, would soon be in her bed.

The two women had not chatted long when the miller's wife once again claimed that she had seen something at the window. Mrs. Shchapoff rose from her chair to investigate, but she was halted in her journey to the window by the sound of an uproar in the attic above their heads. At first it was a flurry of wild rappings that had the two women staring at one another in wide-eyed confusion. Then the pace of the tappings slowed until the sounds became an exact reproduction of the three-step that Maria had been dancing for the child.

"Whatever is that silly woman doing up in the attic." Mrs. Shchapoff frowned. "Has she never her fill of dancing?"

"But how," the miller's wife wanted to know, "could she have got up there without our seeing her pass?"

Without speaking another word, the two women left the sitting room and walked quietly back to the cook's quarters. Opening the door just a crack, they were able to see Maria sound asleep in her bed.

"Then we must see who is in the loft," Mrs. Shchapoff said with determination as she grabbed a lantern from a kitchen shelf.

It had taken a supreme effort of will on the part of the women, but they had managed to walk up the stairs to the attic and shine a light about by way of a rapid examination. The sounds of the dancing continued, but their lantern plainly revealed that there was no one in the loft. Then, as the women beat a hasty retreat from the attic, the rapping seemed to race ahead of them, rattling the windows and pounding at the walls. The miller's wife fled out of the manor to get her husband and the gardener, and Mrs. Shchapoff went to the nursery to check on the welfare of her daughter.

By the time the miller's wife returned with her husband and the gardener, the rappings and the dancing had attained a volume that had roused both Mrs. Shchapoff's mother and her mother-in-law, as well as Maria. The men searched the house and the grounds, but the disturbance continued until dawn.

At 10 o'clock the next night, the dancing ghost once more began its spirited interpretation of the three-step. The house and the grounds were patrolled by servants and neighbors, but the invisible dancer only seemed that much more eager to perform, once again, until dawn.

"I think that you have been into my brandy," Mr. Shchapoff scolded his wife when she had finished telling him the story. He was a sober, no-nonsense landowner and had little patience with stories of ghosts, dancing or otherwise. "Can you ladies substantiate such a wild tale?" he asked his mother and his mother-in-law.

"It is as she says," his mother told him. "Something supernatural has come to this house."

Shchapoff frowned his impatience. "I'm away for a few days and the womenfolk concoct a story that can only frighten the servants and distract them from their work." Gruffly, he sent Maria to fetch the miller, a man Shchapoff regarded as completely sensible and totally reliable.

The miller agreed that the ladies' story was essentially accurate, but he added that he had removed a pigeon's nest from under the cornice of the house. Perhaps the bird had been responsible for the weird noises.

Shchapoff slapped his miller's shoulder and grinned expansively. "Of course that was it! Good man!"

That night, the household retired to their rooms quite early. They were exhausted from their ordeal and felt secure now that the master had returned. Shchapoff bade his family a good night, then sat down to read for a few hours. At about ten o'clock, his attention was distracted by scratching sounds from above his head. That pesky pigeon has come back, he thought. Then, as he listened with close attention, the sounds arranged themselves into the tappings of someone engaged in dancing the three-step.

"Helena is having a bit of fun with me," he grumbled, tossing his book down and stalking up the stairs to his wife's room. He stood outside of her room for just a moment to be certain that he had accurately traced the sound of the dancing. Yes, there was no doubt that the sounds were coming from his wife's room. He pushed open the door and stood ready to deliver a stern lecture to his young wife. She lay in her bed, her eyelids closed in deep sleep. The sounds of dancing had ceased the moment that he had opened the door.

Shchapoff put his hands on his hips and pursed his lips. There was something strange going on here. He had started to close the door when a series of rappings sounded from above his wife's bed. Shchapoff walked quietly to the wall as if he might catch a hidden prankster in the act of hammering on the bedstead. Just as he bent to listen more carefully to the tappings, a rap sounded with such force next to his ear that it nearly deafened him.

His wife sat up in bed, her mouth working on a scream. She calmed when she saw her husband standing near her bedside. "What was that?" she demanded. "Did you hear it?"

"I heard nothing," Shchapoff said, not wanting to alarm his wife. As if to call him a liar, two explosive knocks seemed to shake the very house down to its foundation.

"I'm putting a stop to this," the angry landowner declared, taking his gun from a drawer and slipping n his coat. "I'll get the dogs and the servants, and we'll get whoever is responsible for this outrage!"

Shchapoff found no prankster on whom he might vent his spleen. To those on the outside of the house, the rappings seemed to come from the inside. But those who remained indoors shouted that someone must surely be trying to batter the house down from the outside. At last, Shchapoff had to admit defeat, and he dismissed his men until that morning.

The next day, he enlisted the help of his neighbors as well as his own servants. The crew searched the entire house and examined every foot of the grounds. That night, at Shchapoff's request, his neighbors stayed to witness the disturbances. The invisible guest performed well. It danced above the heads of the searchers all night long, and, for a finale, it struck a door with such force that the heavy wooden planking was nearly torn from the hinges.

By the next night, even Shchapoff was a believer, and it was obvious that he dreaded the onset of a new round of the phenomena. He was pacing the floor nervously until ten o'clock, the time the manifestations usually began. But on this night, there was not a single scratching, rapping, or spritely danced three-step. Nor was there any sound from the loft on the next night. It appeared that things had quieted down in the Shchapoff country house. Or perhaps they might have if Shchapoff would have left well enough alone.

A month later, on December 20th, the Shchapoff's were entertaining guests, who openly expressed their skepticism of the phenomena which their hosts had described as having been active there at the country place. Angrily, Shchapoff summoned Maria to the parlor and commanded her to perform a three-step.

"Probably all the thing needs is a little coaxing and it'll come back," Shchapoff said, ignoring his wife's pleas not to tempt the denizen of the invisible world into returning.

At her master's insistence, Maria danced a brisk little three-step. The cook completed the dance, then looked around the room fearfully as a rapping began at the windows. The assembled guests listened incredulously as they heard an exact repetition of Maria's dance coming from the attic overhead.

"You've planted another servant up there!" someone accused Shchapoff. But when a party went up into the attic, they found no one.

On New Year's Eve, 1871, Shchapoff again ordered Maria to dance a three-step in order to induce the "dancing ghost" to follow her with an act of its own. The country place was filled with guests who heard the echo of Maria's dance coming from the ceiling above their heads. The invisible performer became so animated and enthusiastic that it made some attempts at verbalization with some garbled snatches of Russian folk songs.

Mrs. Shchapoff seemed to offer the poltergeist its energy center. Although well past puberty, Helena Shchapoff was just twenty when the phenomena began.

Perhaps some psychic shock had somehow freed a fragment of her mind from the three dimensional limitations of her main personality, or perhaps a psychic residue in the country place had found a sympathetic energy source in the young woman's psyche. One theory of poltergeistic activity holds that a persistent, dynamic memory or a focus of bottled-up energy in the psychic ether can release itself through a living agent when a person of the right telepathic affinity comes on the scene. This theory seems applicable in the case of the Shchapoff "devil," especially when one learns that phenomena were produced when Mrs. Shchapoff was not present and that the phenomena were localized at the country estate. The disturbances were always reduced or eliminated by a move to the town house in Iletski.

A logical result of having phenomena produced at two holiday parties was, of course, the spreading of stories about the mysterious goings-on at the Shchapoff's country place. Soon, scientists and spiritualists were seeking audience with the "dancing ghost" in widely diverse methods of "communicating" with the strange force.

A Dr. Shustoff explained the whole thing by invoking the magic name of electricity. The soil conditions at the country place, he maintained, produced the weird phenomena. He also theorized that somehow the electrical vibrations might be coming from Mrs. Shchapoff.

Dr. Shustoff's theory of prankish electrical currents was doomed when the phenomena began to give evidence of increasingly advancing intelligence that could respond to conversation and questions advanced by investigators. A Mr. Alekseeff devised a series of knocks which, he claimed, allowed him to communicate with the entity. Mr. Shchapoff had been cursed by the servant of a neighboring miller, according to Mr. Alekseeff. This angry servant had maliciously set a devil on Shchapoff.

The Provincial Governor, General Vervekin, appointed Mr. Akutin, an engineer; the aforementioned Dr. Shustoff, an electrical theorist; and Mr. Savicheff, a magazine editor, to officially investigate the disturbances. This committee decided that Mrs. Shchapoff was producing the effects by means of trickery, and Mr. Shchapoff received a sharply worded letter from the Governor,

47

warning him not to let the "alleged phenomena" recur.

In spite of the Governor's pronunciamento, the disturbances increased in violence at the Shchapoff country place. Now the poltergeist had attained incendiary abilities and Mrs. Shchapoff was once again the one who bore the brunt of the attacks. Balls of fire circled the house and bounced against the windows of her room as if seeking to smash into the house. Dresses that hung unattended in closets burst into flame. A mattress began burning from its underside as a guest readied himself for bed.

The climax of the activity occurred when Mrs. Shchapoff became a veritable pillar of fire in front of the horrified eyes of a house guest and the miller. A crackling noise had come from beneath the floor, followed by a long, high-pitched wailing. A bluish spark seemed to jump up at Mrs. Shchapoff, and her thin dress was instantly swathed in flames. She cried out in terror and collapsed into unconsciousness. The house guest leaped to his feet and valiantly beat the flames out with his bare hands. The most curious thing about the incident was that the courageous guest suffered severe burns while Mrs. Shchapoff received not a single blister, even though her dress was nearly completely consumed by the flames.

The Shchapoffs had had enough of their "dancing ghost." While the entity had contented itself with a nightly performance of the three-step, it had merely been a noisy nuisance. Now the thing had become a terror, quite capable of dealing out firey destruction. Mr. Shchapoff closed up his country place and made arrangements for a permanent move to the city.

The phenomena ceased at once when the Shchapoffs had taken up residence in their town place. Mrs. Shchapoff recovered the health that had been rapidly waning under the onslaughts of the poltergeist. Eight years later, unfortunately, she died in child-birth, but Helena Shchapoff had never suffered an illness after they left the country place.

The Orensburg poltergeist is an unusual case in many ways. Perhaps, as some have theorized, there actually was a curse levied on Mr. Shchapoff by a disgruntled servant of a neighboring miller. The projected hatred of the servant may have intensified what had started out as rather ordinary poltergeistic manifestations (i.e. the rappings at the window, the imitation of the cook's dancing) and transformed them into an agency of malicious evil.

ESTHER COX'S DEMON LOVER

SHE WAS HAVING the dream again, seeing things just as they had been on that terrible night.

Bob had come to pick her up in his buggy. He had only laughed when she had expressed her reluctance at going for a ride when the sky looked so black. "The buggy has a hood that I can raise in case of a shower," he told her.

They had not ridden far when Bob pulled into a small wood outside of Amherst, Nova Scotia. He had wanted her to get down from the buggy and go with him into the wood. She had refused.

Suddenly, Bob had leaped out of the buggy, jerked a pistol from a coat pocket and leveled it at her breast. "You'll come with me into the woods," he threatened, "or I'll kill you!"

"Don't be a fool," she had told him, for she was not lacking in courage. "My honor cannot be purchased by the sight of a madman waving a pistol at me."

Bob had cursed her with a foul stream of profanity. He cocked the hammer of the pistol, and for an awful moment, she wondered if he might not make good his threat. Then there was the sound of wagon wheels creaking toward them. Another couple was seeking out the cover of the wood in which to "spark." Bob thrust the pistol back into a pocket, climbed back into the driver's seat. Sullenly he stared at her, his eyes telling of terrible embarrassment and violent anger. He cracked the reins over the horses' backs and drove at a breakneck speed back toward the village.

On the way home, it had begun to rain. "Please, Bob," she had pleaded. "Put up the cover to keep the rain off us."

As if to punish her for not consenting to appease his lust, Bob pretended not to hear her. He delivered her, soaking wet, to her door at ten that night.

"Wake up, Esther," her sister Jane was shaking her. "You've been dreaming of Bob McNeal again."

Esther Cox began to cry. Bob McNeal had not been seen since the night that he had tried to seduce her. He had not reported for work at the shoe factory that next morning; his landlady said that he had paid for his lodging and left. Evidently shame for what he had tried to do to Esther and fear of the consequences if she told her brother-in-law, who had been Bob's foreman at the factory, had driven him out of Amherst. But Esther had not told her brother-in-law nor her sister Olive nor even Jane. She had kept the memory of that terrible night tightly repressed and bottled up inside her.

"Jane!" Esther whispered harshly. "Do you feel something in bed with us?"

Jane lay still for a moment. "Yes," she answered. "It must be a mouse!"

The two sisters jumped out of bed with a scream and began to search their mattresses. "See there!" Jane said. "Look at the way the straw moves about. He must be making a nest in the straw of the mattress."

The two girls set to beating the mattress vigorously in an attempt to drive the tiny intruder out of their bed, but no mouse retreated from the straw of the mattress. The girls watched the mattress for a bit, detected no further movement, and concluded that the mouse must have escaped without their seeing it.

"We'd better get back to sleep before we wake the rest of the house," Jane suggested. "The "rest of the house" consisted of their brother-in-law, Daniel Teed, who had married their older sister, Olive; the children, Willie and George; John Teed, Daniel's brother; and William Cox, brother of Jane and Esther. The girls decided to make no mention of the "mouse" in their bed, as it would only result in laughter and teasing from the two young men.

The next night, however, the sisters heard a loud scratching from under their bed. They lit a lamp to investigate, and a large cardboard box filled with patchwork jumped out from under the bed. When Jane put it back in its place, it once again leaped into the air. The girls had had enough of trying to deal with the energetic "mouse" and began to call for help.

50

Daniel Teed, groggily slipping on a pair of trousers, answered his sister-in-laws' cries for aid. Grouchily, he kicked the box back under the bed, and it stayed put. He cautioned them about repeating their "little joke."

The girls were quite indignant, when, at breakfast the next morning, they were heartily teased by the whole family. Jane, at twenty-two, and Esther, at eighteen, both felt that they were much too old to be considered empty-headed tricksters.

That night, the disturbances would be much more dramatic and would no longer be considered a joke by the Teed residence. Esther awakened in the night, gasping to her sister that she was dying. Jane lit a lamp, nearly dropped it in horror as she took in the ghastly appearance of her sister. Esther's complexion had become a bright scarlet in color, and her eyes bulged from her skull. Her hair seemed to be standing on end, and her flesh was extremely hot to the touch. Her entire body seemed to be swelling as if someone were inflating her with a pump. Then, while Jane watched in horror, loud thuds and rumbles, like that of thunder, began to sound from the walls of their room.

Daniel and Olive appeared at the door to the girls' room. They had been awakened by the loud reports and wondered what on earth could be their cause. They were shocked at Esther's inflated appearance, then puzzled, when after a particularly violent report, the girl's body seemed to begin deflating. Soon her flesh had returned to normal, and Esther was sleeping peacefully. The family resolved not to say anything of the mysterious disturbances to anyone outside of the household.

Secrecy would soon become an impossibility. That night, the bedclothes flew off the sisters and landed in a heap in a far corner of the room. Esther once again began to swell, and when John Teed came to investigate, a pillow shot from the bed and struck him full in the face. The young man could not be coaxed to re-enter the room, but the remainder of the household sat on the edge of the bed, straining their individual bulks and strengths to keep the blankets over the swollen Esther. While they fought with the bedclothes, a series of sharp explosions began to sound about the room; and,

51

as the reports crashed and banged, Esther began to deflate just as she had done the night before.

Daniel Teed resolved that he would be ready on the next night and had their family physician, Dr. Caritte, in attendance. The doctor examined Esther, and, while he felt her pulse, stated that the girl seemed to be suffering from some kind of nervous shock. His words seemed to be the signal for which the phenomena had been waiting. Esther's pillow straightened out as if it were a balloon suddenly filled with air. John Teed grasped for it, and the pillow deflated itself. When it re-inflated itself, the younger Teed got hold of it; but the pillow wrenched itself from his closed fists as if it were alive.

The assembled household and Dr. Caritte were next attracted to the sounds of scratching on the wall above Esther's bed. Incredulously, they witnessed writing forming on the plaster. "Esther Cox," wrote the invisible hand, "you are mine to kill."

Dr. Caritte returned the next evening with a powerful sedative for the afflicted young woman. He admitted that the phenomena was beyond his medical knowledge, but he concluded that as Esther seemed to experience the symptoms of nervous excitement, the only thing that he could prescribe would be sedation. Dr. Caritte's suggested bromide had a completely opposite effect than the one for which he had hoped. As soon as the drug had eased Esther in a deep slumber, the noises began, louder than they had ever been. It sounded as though someone were on the roof, attempting to pound his way into the house by means of a heavy sledgehammer. The doctor retreated shortly after midnight, and as he walked away down the street, he could still hear the powerful blows shaking the Teed home.

The disturbances continued in this manner for three weeks, with Dr. Caritte attending Esther three times a day in vain attempts to help her. Then, one night, the girl fell into a trance and spewed out the whole story of Bob McNeal's attempted assault on her honor. The family had known nothing of Esther's secret until that moment. When she regained consciousness, Jane told her what she had said, and Esther confessed that it was all true.

"Could it be," Olive wondered, "that Bob McNeal was killed or took his own life and has come back to haunt Esther?"

As if on cue, three loud knocks sounded on the bedroom wall. Jane was slightly conversant with spiritism and suggested that whatever it was that had been bothering her sister might be trying to establish contact with them. This comment, too, was met by the thudding of three raps.

Dr. Caritte quickly devised a simple code. One rap was to represent "no," two raps would signify "no answer" or "doubtful," and three raps would stand for "yes." The "ghost" used the code to answer elementary questions put forth by the household, but ignored all attempts on the part of Dr. Caritte to establish a pattern of clues to its existence.

By now, the secret of the phenomena could no longer be confined to the walls of the Teed home. For one thing, neighbors and passers-by had heard the strange poundings and had inquired as to their cause. Village clergymen began either to fulminate against Esther from their pulpits or to defend her. The Teeds' minister, Reverend A. Temple of the Wesleyan Methodist Church, had himself witnessed a pail of cold water suddenly begin to boil in Esther's presence.

Daniel Teed had just applied for police protection to keep the curious from turning his home into a "public resort," when Esther contacted diptheria and all manifestations ceased for a period of two weeks. Upon her recovery, she was sent to recuperate from her illness at the home of Mrs. Snowden, another married sister, who lived at Sackville, New Brunswick. There was no return of the phenomena throughout the duration of her stay.

"Let's hope you're cured of whatever ailed you," Daniel Teed sighed upon his sister-in-law's return to his home. He had never been very sympathetic to Esther during the onslaught of the mysterious phenomena and had seemed more concerned about "what the neighbors would say" than he had been about her health. "Just to be sure, though," he added, "we're giving you and Jane a new room to see that you get a fresh start."

Esther had only been home one night when lighted matches began to fall from the ceiling. All of the tiny flames were extinguished, but the incendiary activity was by no means ended. Rappings began to sound on the walls, and by using the code that Dr. Caritte had developed, the family learned that the entity intended to set their house on fire. As if to signal that it meant business, a dress jumped from its place on a nail and burst into flames as it slid under Esther's bed.

For three days, the entire household kept vigil against the "spirit's" threat of destroying their home. Just when they thought that the threat might have been an idle one after all, Olive smelled smoke coming from the cellar. Grabbing one of the buckets of water that they had kept at the ready, she and Esther found a pile of wood shavings blazing in a corner. The contents of the bucket seemed to have little effect on the flames. The sisters fled from the house, screaming for help, and ran into a passing stranger, who fortunately had enough presence of mind to beat the fire out with a doormat.

"Rappings are one thing," Daniel Teed decreed that night at dinner, "but fires are something else. If our house caught fire and the wind was right, half of the town of Amherst would go up in smoke. I'm sorry, Esther, but I just can't let you stay here any longer."

Olive looked askance at her husband, but there was little that she could say. He had, after all, been remarkably patient with his sister-in-law.

John W. White offered to employ Esther in his restaurant and provide lodging for her. "Maybe she just needs to get out of the house," White said hopefully.

The well-meaning Mr. White soon regretted his decision to come to Esther's aid. The heavy door of his large kitchen stove refused to stay closed, even when braced by an axe handle. Metal objects clung to Esther's body as if she were a living magnet. Metal utensils, which came into contact with her flesh, became too hot for customers to hold. The furniture shifted about regularly, and a fifty-pound box once shot fifteen feet into the air.

"She's ruining my business," John White appealed to Daniel Teed. "I've no choice but to send her back to you."

A Captain James Beck invited Esther to come to stay a time with him and his wife at St. John, New Brunswick. He had read of the "Amherst Mystery" and wished to study the alleged agent of the phenomena at leisure and in his own home. Esther proved to be a big disappointment to Captain Beck and the groups of medical men and scientists which had gathered to examine her. For three weeks, the girl did nothing other than tell wild tales of three ghosts, "Peter Cox," "Maggie Fisher," and "Bob Nickle," who appeared regularly to threaten her with fires and stabbings.

Upon her return to Amherst, Esther spent another quiet sojourn at the farm of a Mr. and Mrs. Van Ambergh. It was deemed that all traces of the phenomena had at last left her, and she was once again welcomed back into the home of Daniel Teed. Unfortunately, Esther had barely unpacked her things when the disturbances began with renewed vigor.

Teed was at the "grasping at straws" stage when a magician named Walter Hubbell offered not only to attempt to "lay" the ghost that afflicted Esther but also to pay rent if he might stay in the house and observe the disturbances at firsthand. The day that Hubbell, as star boarder, moved in with the Teeds marked a particularly violent onset of the phenomena. His umbrella was jerked out of his hand and tossed into the air. A large butcher knife appeared and menacingly headed in his direction. Whenever he entered a room, all the chairs therein would fall over or dance about noisily.

"The ghosts don't like you," Esther said finally, by way of understatement.

Hubbell was undaunted, even pleased, that the manifestations had become so robust since his arrival. Throughout his stay of about five weeks, Hubbell witnessed a *pot pourri* of poltergeistic activity, such as the spirits whistling and drumming "Yankee Doodle," the extremely active behavior of the furniture, the blasting of an invisible trumpet, and the subsequent materialization of the trumpet in very tangible German silver.

His stay in the Teed home was not without its dangers. Several knifes were thrown at him, a large glass paperweight narrowly missed his head, and a variety of bruises were sustained on his limbs by the boisterous activity of the dancing furniture. Esther, too, seemed to suffer more personal attacks after the paying observer had arrived. Once, thirty pins materialized out of the air and drove themselves into different parts of her body. Another time, after returning from church, her head was cut open by an old bone that had been lying in the yard.

Hubbell had not been quite honest with the Teeds when he had told them that he wished only to observe the disturbances. As an accomplished stage magician, the man had found himself completely awed by the girl's ability to produce genuine phenomena. It wasn't long before he was envisioning Esther on tour, with himself as her manager. At the same time, he was taking copious notes for a book which he intended to write on the Amherst mystery.

It didn't take Hubbell more than a few hours to convince Daniel Teed that he should be permitted to make all the arrangements necessary to put his sister-in-law on the stage. Olive and Jane objected to the placing of their sister on public display, but Teed squelched all arguments by pointing out that their home was in a shambles.

"Esther has caused all this destruction by setting her ghosts loose on us," Teed complained. "It's only right that she should pay us back in some way for all the grief she's caused this family."

The end of grief was not yet in sight. Walter Hubbell rented a large auditorium and sold tickets to a curious crowd who had come to see Esther produce "wonders and miracles" on the stage. The stage debut of Esther Cox was a disaster. Not a single supernormal act took place, and the restive audience was soon chanting for the return of their money.

Daniel Teed had endured his last humiliation. He ordered both Esther and Hubbell from his home. The magician shrugged his shoulders and left for St. John, New Brunswick to begin writing his book on the "haunting." Esther was at last taken in by the Van Amberghs, who had not suffered from her last visit and had grown fond of the girl.

Shortly before the publication of the book on the Amherst mystery, Hubbell tried to contact Esther Cox by mail. He was shocked to receive a letter from her sister, Jane, informing him that the unfortunate girl was serving a jail sentence for arson. She had been charged with "burning the barn" of some farmers named Davidson, for whom she had been working as a servant girl. This was the last record of her manifestations.

Walter Hubbell's book, published during the latter part of 1879, was an instantaneous success; and, by 1916, the "true ghost story" had gone into ten editions. The magician had accomplished what he had set out to do: make a great deal of money on someone else's "magic."

POSSESSED BY THE POLTERGEIST

"Sir," Mr. Webster addressed his tenant, Captain Molesworth, "why do you persist in accusing me of the extraordinary noises and disturbances which take place in your home? I am your landlord and the house belongs to me. For what reason should I wish to drive you out and give my house such a bad reputation that no one else would ever again occupy it?"

Captain Molesworth scowled. "If you are not the human agency responsible for the noise and knockings, then you should have warned me that the place was haunted!"

"There were no disturbances in the house before you moved in," Webster retorted. "I believe that your young daughter is involved in some sort of trickery. Surely there are no ghosts in 1835!"

Captain Molesworth once again stormed out of his landlord's study without gaining the slightest bit of satisfaction. In fact, their heated discussion had ended with Mr. Webster's threatening to take him to court for the damage done to the house. The landlord had found it very difficult to believe that some invisible agency was responsible for ripping up floorboards, knocking holes in walls, or scorching furniture with fire.

Whether Mr. Webster would believe it or not, Captain Molesworth knew that he would have to go home to face the incessant sound of invisible feet parading about the bed of his invalid daughter and the maddening knocking that seemed to throb in rhythm to some nameless tune.

Certain friends claimed that the spirit of his deceased daughter, Martha, had come back to wear down the last reserves of her sister Jane so that the sickly girl might join her beyond the grave. Others theorized that the spirit of Martha was attempting to possess the body of Jane and attain a zombie-like existence.

Captain Molesworth enlisted the aid of law enforcement officers, masons, justices of the peace, and army officers to help him snare the "ghost" that gave him and his daughter not a moment's rest. Because the phenomena was most active around the bed of the twelve-year-old Jane, the unfortunate girl was subjected to all sorts of cruel examinations. Once she was even bound up in a heavy cloth bag for a period of several hours.

The frail young girl was undoubtedly hastened into the other world more by the severe measures taken by the amateur investigators than by any returning "ghost," but it is of no surprise to learn that the phenomena ceased upon Jane's death.

It is at this point that an alternate theory of poltergeists may be presented. There are those who maintain that the disturbances which some researchers ascribe to "projected repressions" or "fragments of a living personality" are actually caused by ghosts or demons. From their point of view, the person who has become the energy center for poltergeistic phenomena is, in reality, in rapport with or under the control of one or the other of these inhabitants of the invisible realm.

Those who espouse this theory hold it a great error to suppose that the Scriptural term "possessed by a devil" was but a euphemism for mental illness. Nor, they believe, is it correct to assume that demonic possession cannot occur after the Resurrection of Christ. Therefore, following this line of thought, the inexplicable motion of objects, the materialization of water and solid materials, the blasphemous voices, the infantile and obscene behavior of the phenomena are all a result of temporary possession by ghost or demon.

MARY JOBSON'S STRANGE VOICES

It was between her twelfth and thirteenth year, in November of 1839, that young Mary Jobson began to suffer from the strange illness that afflicted her frail body for nearly eleven weeks. To add to their concern while they attended their sick daughter, Mr. and Mrs. Jobson were puzzled to hear the sound of rapping coming from the area of Mary's bed. At first, they had thought that the child pounded at the bedstead while in the delerium of her fever, but they had been in the room and had heard the knocking while her hands were plainly in view.

The rappings had been but a very elementary beginning of the phenomena that were about to manifest themselves in the Jobson home. A strange, whispering voice, that seemed to come from nowhere in particular, began to predict events in their family circle which later proved to be accurate. The knockings had matured into violent explosions and such loud rumblings that the tenant below Mary's room often yelled up that he feared the ceiling was about to crash down on him. Footsteps stomped loudly about Mary's bed, closet doors opened of their own accord, water seemed to fall from the ceiling, and, strangest of all, an invisible organ began to play sweet and ethereal music.

The Jobson's family doctor retained his skepticism about the phenomena, as did John Jobson, but the manifestations, especially the "heavenly" voice, began to attract wide attention. The voice declared that "it" was good and was able to administer good advice to those who came to hear it.

Mary's teacher, Elizabeth Gauntlett, was summoned by the voice while she was doing housework in her own home. "Elizabeth Gauntlett, one of your scholars is sick," the voice said. "Go and see her; and it will be good for you." Miss Gauntlett obeyed the voice, inquired as to the address of her pupil, and received "many marvelous signs" at the bedside of the young girl.

The voice revealed to the distraught parents that their child had been temporarily "possessed" by a "good

59

spirit." They were told that "though Mary appears to suffer, she does not. She does not know where her body is. Her own spirit has left this body, and I have entered it."

The girl's bedroom became a sort of shrine as the girl's body became a "speaking-trumpet" for the voices of departed friends and loved ones and the revelations of the "good spirit."

"Look up, and you shall see the sun and moon on the ceiling!" the voice once said. Before the bewildered eyes of a roomful of witnesses, a beautiful representation of the celestial orbs appeared in lively colors of yellow and orange. John Jobson immediately set about whitewashing the figures, but he soon learned that the voice had intended that its artwork be permanent. He put his brushes away when he discovered, after several coats of whitewash, that the figures still remained visible.

Perhaps the most astounding materialization affected by this peculiar poltergeist was that of a lamb, which was witnessed by Margaret Watson. The skeptical father once demanded another physical sign of the voice and received a large quantity of water dumped at his feet. He called for more water, and another deluge was forthcoming. Again, he called and again and again, until he had commanded the appearance of water a full twenty times, and the bedroom was drenched.

The celestial music that attended this poltergeist is most intriguing. Not only did the sound of a melodious organ continually fill the room with strains of hymns, but on several occasions, lovely voices of an invisible choir sang to its accompaniment.

In spite of the voice's assurances that Mary Jobson was not really suffering, her young frame continued to give every evidence of an extremely long convalescence. At last, the voice announced that Mary Jobson would be the recipient of a miracle which would be wrought on June 22nd. Their doctor advised the Jobsons that the miracle would come none too soon. Mary was as ill as ever, and, if the strange, undefined disease continued this peculiar course, death would be imminent.

When the appointed day arrived, Mary's strength seemed to be rapidly diminishing. Her fever had risen, and the doctor was not optimistic about the girl's chances of seeing another day. At five o'clock, the voice instructed Mrs. Jobson to lay out some clothes for Mary. Too dazed by grief and worry to refuse, the woman did as she had been told. After this was done, the voice ordered everyone from the bedroom with the exception of Mary's two-year-old brother.

The Jobsons and the doctor spent an anxious fifteen minutes outside the door of Mary's room before they heard the voice cry: "Come in!" When they entered the room, Mary sat smiling in a chair, completely dressed, bouncing her baby brother on her knee. From that moment on, she seldom suffered from any illness and never received another visitation from the "good spirit." She matured into a very well-educated and highly respected young woman. In spite of "an undetermined disease of the brain" which lasted for seven months, Mary Jobson apparently suffered no psychic scars from her most unusual poltergeist.

THE VICIOUS DEVIL OF BORLEY

WHEN THE Reverend Mr. Brown opened the cabinet in the library to put away some books, he was startled to see a human skull grinning at him from a shelf.

"I say, dear," he called to his wife after he had recovered from his shock, "come look at this."

Mrs. Brown sucked in her breath as her husband removed the skull from the cabinet and began to examine it. "You don't suppose," she asked with nervous laughter, "that the rectory really is haunted?"

Reverend Brown smiled. "More than likely, the rector who preceded us here had an unusual taste in paperweights."

"You don't think that could be the skull of the nun that's supposed to walk through these halls," Mrs. Brown persisted, "or the skull of one of the poor devils that was buried in the Plague Pit?"

"Easy now," her husband cautioned, "or you'll have yourself believing all the weird tales we've heard about Borley Rectory."

"But you cannot deny the fact that no fewer than a dozen clergymen refused to live here before you accepted the call," Mrs. Brown said. "Nor can you deny that a former rector had that window in the dining room bricked up because he could not stand to see the ghost of the nun continually peering in at him."

Reverend Brown tried to ignore his wife's suggestion that "something evil" had made its abode in the rectory. He and the sexton gave the skull a solemn burial in the churchyard, and he and his wife fought to stave off the depression that seemed to have enveloped them. It was not many nights, however, before they were given awesome evidence of invisible forces at work.

It usually began shortly after they had retired for the evening. They would be lying in bed, and they would hear the sound of heavy footsteps walking past their door. Mr. Brown soon took to crouching in the darkness outside of their room with a hockey stick gripped firmly in his hands. Several nights he lunged at "something" that passed their door—always without result.

Bells began to ring at all hours and became an intolerable nuisance. Hoarse, inaudible whispers sounded over their heads. Small pebbles appeared from nowhere to pelt them. A woman's voice began to moan from the center of an arch leading to the chapel. Keys popped from their locks and were found several feet from their doors. The Browns had found themselves living in what Dr. Harry Price would soon come to call "the most haunted house in England."

In the summer of 1929, Dr. Price answered the plea of the haunted rector and his wife. Leaving London, Dr. Price and an assistant drove to the small village of Borley, reviewing what they already knew about the eerie Rectory. The building, though constructed in modern times, stood on the site of a medieval monastery whose gloomy old vaults still lay beneath it. Close at hand had been a nunnery, whose ruins were much in evidence. About a quarter of a mile away, stood a castle where many tragic events had occurred, ending with a seige by Oliver Cromwell. There was a persistent legend about a nun who had been walled up alive in the nunnery for eloping with a lay brother who had been employed at the monastery. The lay brother, who received the punishment meted out for such sins, was hanged. Inhabitants of the Rectory, and several villagers, had reported seeing the veiled nun walking a path through the grounds. A headless nobleman and a black coach pursued by armed men had also been listed as a frequent phenomenon.

The present Rectory had been built in 1865 by the Rev. Henry Martin. He had fathered fourteen children and had wanted a large rectory. He died in the Blue Room in 1892 and was succeeded in occupancy by his son, Lionel, who died at the Rectory in 1927. The building was vacant for a few months—while a dozen clergymen refused to take up residence there because of the eerie tales which they had heard—until Reverend George Brown and his family accepted the call in 1928.

The psychical researcher did not have to wait long for the phenomena to put on a show for him. Price and his assistant had just shared a lunch with Mr. and Mrs. Brown when a glass candlestick struck an iron stove near the investigator's head and splashed him with splinters. A mothball came tumbling down the stairwell, followed by a number of pebbles.

Price busied himself for the next several days with interviewing the surviving daughters of Henry Martin, the builder of the Rectory, and as many former servants as had remained in the village. The eldest of the three surviving daughters told of seeing the nun appear at a lawn party on a sunny July afternoon. She had approached the phantom and tried to engage it in conversation, but it had disappeared as she had drawn near to it. The sisters swore that the entire family had often seen the nun and the phantom coach and that their brother, Lionel, had said that, when dead, he would attempt to manifest himself in the same way. It was their father, Henry Martin, who had bricked up the dining room window so that the family might eat in peace and not be disturbed by the spectral nun peeping in at them.

A man who had served as gardener for the Martin family told Price that every night for eight months he and his wife heard footsteps in their rooms over the stables. Several former maids or grooms testified that they had remained in the employ of the Martins for only one or two days before they were driven away by the

63

strange occurrences which manifested themselves on the premises.

Mrs. Brown was not at all reluctant to admit that she, too, had seen the shadowy figure of a nun walking about the grounds of the Rectory. On several occasions, she had hurried to confront the phantom, but it had always disappeared at the sound of her approach.

The Browns left the Rectory shortly after Dr. Price's visit. They had both begun to suffer the ill-effects of the lack of sleep and the enormous mental strain which had been placed on each of them.

Borley Rectory presents an interesting combination of a "haunting" and the phenomenon of poltergeistic activity. Harry Price maintained that approximately one-half of all hauntings include some type of poltergeistic disturbance. There are those, of course, who will use such cases to "prove" their supposition that the poltergeist is truly a racketing ghost. Others will point out the possibility that whatever facet of mind is capable of producing the phenomena of the poltergeist may also be capable of activating the subconscious memory patterns of the dead that, in some way not yet known to science, have been impressed on the psychic ether. A child approaching puberty may be of just the proper telepathic affinity to allow these bottled-up memories to release their energy through the medium of his own fragmented psyche.

Henry Martin had fourteen children who lived in the Rectory. Phenomena began to become active about ten years after he had moved into the Rectory with his family. It is also interesting to record that the phenomena reached new heights of activity when the Rev. B. Morrison took up residence in the Rectory on October 16, 1930. The Reverend brought with him his wife, Marianne, and his twelve-year-old daughter.

The Morrisons had lived there only a few days when Mrs. Morrison heard a voice softly calling, "Marianne, dear." The words were repeated many times, and, thinking her husband was summoning her, Mrs. Morrison ran upstairs. Mr. Morrison had not spoken a word, he told her, but he, too, had heard the calling voice.

Once, Mrs. Morrison laid her wristwatch by her side as she prepared to wash herself in the bathroom. When

64

she completed her washing, she reached for the watch and discovered that the band had been removed. It was never returned.

Reverend Morrison was quick to realize that the weird tales that he had heard about Borley Rectory had all been true. He could hardly deny them in view of such dramatic evidence. He was not frightened, however, as he felt protected by his Christian faith. He used a holy relic to quiet the disturbances when they became particularly violent and remained calm enough to keep a detailed journal of the phenomena which he and his family witnessed.

Mrs. Marianne Morrison received the full fury of the poltergeist's attack from the very beginning of their occupancy. One night, while carrying a candle on the way to their bedroom, she received such a violent blow in the eye that it produced a cut and a black bruise which was visible for several days. A hammer-head was thrown at her one night as she prepared for bed. She received a blow from a piece of metal that was hurled down a flight of stairs. Another time, Mrs. Morrison narrowly missed being struck by a flat iron, which smashed the chimney of the lamp that she was carrying.

In addition to persecuting Mrs. Morrison, the poltergeist seemed determined to establish contact with her. Messages were found scrawled on the walls: "Marianne—please—get help."

The poltergeist may or may not have been suggesting that the Morrisons once again bring Dr. Harry Price upon the scene. At any rate, that is exactly what they did. Advised by the Martin sisters of the famed investigator's interest in the Borley phenomena, Reverend Morrison wrote to London to inform Dr. Price of renewed activity in the Rectory.

Price gained permission to stay in the Rectory with two friends and set out at once for the village. Upon arrival, the researcher and his party once again examined the house from attic to cellar. The phenomena wasted no time in welcoming the returning investigator. While he was examining an upstairs room, an empty wine bottle hurled itself through the air, narrowly missing him. The party was brought back down to the kitchen by the screams of their chauffeur, who had remained behind to enjoy a leisurely smoke. The distraught man insisted that he had seen a large, black hand crawl across the kitchen floor.

During conversation, Mrs. Morrison disclosed that she had seen the "monster" that had been causing all the eerie disturbances. Reverend Morrison showed Dr. Price the entry that he had made in his journal on March 28th when his wife had confronted the entity while ascending a staircase. She had described it as a monstrosity —black, ugly, ape-like. It had reached out and touched her on the shoulder with an "iron-like touch." Price later learned that others had seen the creature on different occasions.

The Morrisons also told Price and his team that the phenomena had begun to produce items which they had never seen before. A small tin trunk had appeared in the kitchen when the family was eating supper. A powder box and a wedding ring materialized in the bathroom, and, after they had been put away in a drawer, the ring disappeared over night. Stone-throwing had become common, and Reverend Morrison complained of finding stones in their bed and under their pillows as well.

Although Reverend Morrison was a brave man, he had never enjoyed good health nor the kind of stamina necessary to outlast a poltergeist. It is, of course, a tribute to the family to record that they did stick it out at the Rectory for five years before leaving in October of 1935. After the Morrisons had raised the white-flag of surrender to the phenomena, the Bishop wisely decreed that the place was put up for sale, and it should have come as no surprise to the parish to discover that there would be no interested parties waiting in line to bid on it.

In May of 1937, Harry Price learned that the Rectory was empty and offered to rent the place as a type of "ghost" laboratory. His sum was accepted, and the investigator enlisted a crew of forty men who would take turns living in the Rectory for a period of one year. Price outfitted the place and issued a booklet which told his army of researchers how to correctly observe and record any phenomena which might manifest itself.

Shortly after the investigators began to arrive, strange pencil-like writings began to appear on the walls. Each time a new marking was discovered, it would be carefully circled and dated. Two Oxford graduates reported seeing new writing form while they were busy ringing and dating another. It appeared that the entity missed Mrs. Morrison. "Marianne . . . Marianne . . . M . . ." it wrote over and over again. "Marianne . . . light . . . Mass . . . prayers"; "Get lights"; "Marianne . . . please . . . help . . . get."

The organized investigators were quick to discover a phenomenon which had not been noted by any of the Rectors who had lived in Borley. This was the location of a "cold spot" in one of the upstairs passages. Certain people began to shiver and feel faint whenever they passed through it. Another "cold spot" was discovered on the landing outside of the Blue Room. Thermometers indicated the temperature of these areas to be fixed at about 48-degrees, regardless of what the temperature of the rest of the house may have been.

The "nun" was seen three times in one evening by one observer, but was not noticed at all by any of the other investigators. A strange old cloak kept the researchers baffled by continually appearing and disappearing. Several of Price's crew reported being touched by unseen hands.

On the last day of Dr. Price's tenancy, the wedding ring once again materialized. The investigator snatched it up, lest it disappear, and brought it home to London with him.

Professor C. E. M. Joad, of the Department of Philosophy and Psychology at the University of London was one of those who witnessed the pencil markings appearing on the walls. In the July, 1938 issue of *Harper's Magazine,* Professor Joad commented on this experience. ". . . having reflected long and carefully upon that squiggle I did not and do not see how it could have been made by normal means. . . . The hypothesis that poltergeister materialize lead pencils and fingers to use them seems to be totally incredible. . . . And the question of 'why' seems hardly less difficult to answer than the question 'how.' As so frequently occurs when one is investigating so-called abnormal phenomena, one finds it equally impossible to withhold credence from the facts or to credit any possible explanation of the facts. Either the facts did not occur, or if they did, the universe must in some respects be totally other than what one is accustomed to suppose."

In late 1939, the Borley Rectory was purchased by a Captain W. H. Gregson, who renamed it "The Priory." He was not at all disturbed by warnings that the place was haunted, but he was upset when his faithful old dog went wild with terror on the day they moved in and ran away never to be seen again. He was also mildly concerned with the strange track of unidentified footprints that circled the house in fresh fallen snow. They were not caused by any known animal, the captain swore, nor had any man made them. He followed the tracks for a time until they mysteriously disappeared into nothingness.

Captain Gregson did not have long to puzzle out the enigma of Borley. At midnight of February 27, 1939, the "most haunted house in England" was completely gutted by flames. Captain Gregson testified later that a number of books had flown from their places on the shelves and knocked over a lamp, which had immediately exploded into flame.

THE DISRESPECTFUL POLTERGEIST OF EPWORTH

As WE HAVE SEEN, the poltergeist is no respector of persons. One of the most famous poltergeists in the annals of noisy hauntings is the one that visited the Reverend Samuel Wesley and his family at Epworth Rectory in 1716. Among the nineteen children of the Reverend Wesley who witnessed the phenomena were John and Charles, the founders of Methodism and the authors of some of Christendom's best loved hymns.

It was on the first of December that the children and the servants began to complain of eerie groans and mysterious knockings in their rooms. They also insisted that they could hear the sound of footsteps ascending and descending the stairs at all hours of the night.

Reverend Wesley heard no noises for about a week and severely lectured the child or servant who brought him any wild tale about a ghost walking about in the Rectory.

"If there are noises in the Rectory," he told his family one night at dinner, "they are undoubtedly caused by the silly young men who come around here in the evenings."

The Reverend had four grown daughters who had begun to entertain beaus and suitors, and their father's veiled sarcasm did not sit at all well with them. "I wish the ghost would come knocking at your door, Father," one of them told him, blushing furiously at her own boldness.

The girls were so angry with their father that they fought down their fright and vowed to ignore the noises until they became so loud that their no-nonsense parent could not help acknowledging them.

They didn't have long to wait. The very next night, nine loud knocks thudded on the walls of Reverend Wesley's bed chamber.

"Someone has managed to get into the Rectory unnoticed and is trying to frighten us," Wesley whispered to his wife. "Tomorrow I'll buy a dog big enough to gobble up any intruder!"

True to his word, the clergyman obtained a huge mastiff and brought it into the Rectory. "This brute will deal with your spook," he told his children.

That night, however, as the knocks began to sound, Reverend Wesley was startled to see his canine bodyguard whimper and cower behind the frightened children.

"He's more frightened than we are, Father," one of the older girls teased.

Two nights later, the sounds in the house seemed so violent that Wesley and his wife were forced out of bed to investigate. As they walked through the rectory, the noises seemed to play about them. Mysterious crashing sounds echoed in the darkness. Metallic clinks seemed to fall in front of them. Somehow managing to maintain their courage, the Wesleys searched every chamber but found nothing.

After he called a family meeting to pool their knowledge about the invisible guest, Reverend Wesley learned from one of the older girl's observations that the disturbances usually began at about ten o'clock in the evening and were always prefaced by a "signal" noise, like the "strong winding up of a jack." The noises followed a pattern that seldom varied. They would begin in the kitchen, then suddenly fly up to visit a bed, knocking first at the foot, then the head. These seemed to be the ghost's "warming-up exercises." After it had followed these preliminaries, it might indulge any spectral whim which appealed to it on that particular night.

"Why do you disturb innocent children?" Wesley roared in righteous indignation one night as the knockings in the nursery became especially violent. "If you have something to say, come to me in my study!"

The thing seemed to ignore the clergyman and continued to bang about on the bedsteads of the children.

"You deaf and dumb devil, why do you frighten these children that cannot answer for themselves? Come to me in my study like a man!"

As if in answer to Wesley's challenge, a knock sounded on the door of his study with such force that the cleric thought the boards must surely have been shattered.

Although there were no more disturbances that evening, the cleric soon found out that his invitation to come to the study had not been ignored. Once he was pushed heavily against his desk "by an invisible power," and another time he was slammed into the door jamb of his study just as he was entering.

Wesley decided to secure reinforcements in the fight against the "deaf and dumb devil" which had invaded his rectory. He sent for Mr. Hoole, the Vicar of Hoxley, and told him the whole story.

Mr. Hoole listened patiently to his fellow cleric's story, his eyes subtly flicking over Wesley's face for signs of overwork and tension. "I shall lead devotions tonight," he told the Rector of Epworth, "and see if the thing will dare to manifest itself in my presence."

The "thing" was not the least bit awed by the Vicar of Hoxley. In fact, it put on such a good show that night that the clergyman fled in terror, leaving Wesley to combat the "demon" as best he could.

The children had overcome their initial fear of the invisible being and had come to accept its antics as a welcome relief from the boredom of village life. "Old

Jeffery," as they had begun to call their strange guest, had almost achieved the status of a pet.

Old Jeffery, it was soon observed, was quite sensitive. If any visitor slighted him by claiming that the rappings were due to natural causes, such as rats, birds or wind, the phenomena were quickly intensified so that the doubter stood instantly corrected.

The disturbances maintained their scheduled arrival time of about ten o'clock in the evening until the day that Mrs. Wesley remembered the ancient remedy for riding a house of evil spirits.

"We'll get a large trumpet," she told the family, "and blow it mightily throughout every room in the house. The sounds of a loud horn are unpleasing to evil spirits."

The ear-splitting experiment in exorcism was not only a complete failure, but now the "spirit" began to manifest itself in the daylight as well. Old Jeffery had either resented the charge of being an "evil spirit" or else it was simply expressing its criticism of the terrible trumpeting by retaliating with increased activity.

The children seemed almost to welcome the fact that Old Jeffery would be available during their playtime hours as well as being an amusing nighttime nuisance. Several witnesses reported seeing a bed levitate itself to a considerable height while a number of the Wesley children squealed gaily from the floating mattress. The only thing that bothered the children was the creepy sound, like that of a trailing robe, that Old Jeffery had begun to make. Hetty declared that she had seen the ghost of a man in a long, white robe that dragged on the floor. Other children claimed to have seen an animal, similar in appearance to a badger, scurrying out from under their beds. The servants swore that they had seen the head of a rodent-like creature peering out at them from a crack near the kitchen fireplace.

Then, just as the Wesleys were getting accustomed to their weird visitor, the disturbances ended as abruptly as they had begun. Old Jeffery never returned to plague Epworth Rectory with its phenomena, but the memory of its occupancy has remained to bewilder scholars of more than two centuries.

71

OCCASIONALLY, when one is stalking the poltergeist, he comes across a case where a sinister force from the past maintains a firm hold on a dwelling and exerts a dramatic influence on all those who occupy it. Such was the phenomena that gripped Hinton Ampner.

The most complete account of the disturbances was set down in her own hand by Mrs. Mary Ricketts, who, with her children, servants, and her brother, had been a witness to manifestations of a most eerie and frightening sort. The whole Hinton Ampner case was written up in the *Journal of the Society for Psychical Research,* for April, 1893.

Mary Ricketts was no gullible female. She was intelligent, widely read, and her reputation for truthfulness forever went unsullied. Her brother, John Jervis, was created Baron Jervis and Earl St. Vincent for his distinguished naval services. In 1757, Mary had married William Henry Ricketts of Canaan, Jamaica. For several years, she had accompanied her husband on his frequent business trips to the West Indies, but, in 1769, having now mothered three children, she decided to remain alone in England at the old manor house that they occupied.

From the very first there had been disturbances— sound of doors slamming, the shuffling of footsteps. Mr. Ricketts had spent many nights watching for the "prowlers" that he was convinced had somehow gained entrance into the country place. They had lived at Hinton Ampner for about six-months before their nurse "plainly saw a gentleman in a drab-colored suit of clothes go into the yellow room."

Such things the Ricketts tolerated for four years, firmly convinced that the noises were the result of wind and prowlers, and the gray man—and a once sighted figure of a woman—were the products of the superstitions and fears to which "the lower class of people are so prone." Because they were convinced of a natural explanation for the disturbances, William had no pronounced anxiety when Mary told him that she felt that she should remain in England with the children while he made the trip to Jamaica. After all, she did have eight servants to assist her, and it was quite unlikely that any prowler would try to take on such odds.

The phenomena seemed almost to have been waiting for Mr. Ricketts to leave on an extended trip before it began its manifestations in earnest. He had only been gone a short time when, one afternoon while lying down in her room, Mary heard the noise of someone walking in the room and the rustling of silk clothing as it brushed the floor. She opened her eyes to see no one—absolutely no one. She called the servants and a thorough search was made of the upstairs rooms and closets. The cook reminded her mistress that she had heard the same rustling noise descending the stairs on several occasions and had once seen the tall figure of a woman in dark clothes. Mrs. Ricketts found herself doing less pooh-poohing of the servants' stories now that she, too, had heard the spectral rustling of an invisible lady.

Nocturnal noises continued, and, one night, as Mary Ricketts lay sleeping in the yellow room which the "gray man" had been seen to enter, she was awakened by the heavy plodding steps of a man walking toward the foot of her bed. She was too frightened to reach for the bell at her bedside. She jumped from her bed and ran from the room into the nursery. The children's nurse was instantly out of her bed, rubbing her sleep-swollen eyes and wondering what on earth had so upset the mistress of the house. The nurse became immediately awake when Mary Ricketts told her about the plodding footsteps. The rest of the servants were summoned and again a fruitless search was made to discover some human agency who might be responsible for the disturbance.

It was in November that the knocking and rappings began. A few months later, after the first of the year, Mrs. Ricketts and her household noticed that the entire house seemed to be filled with the sound of a "hollow murmuring." A maid, who had spent the night in the yellow room, appeared at the breakfast table pale-faced and shaken over the "dismal groans and fluttering" that she had heard around her bed most of the night.

By midsummer the voices were intolerable. Mrs. Ricketts wrote: "They began before I went to bed, and with intermissions were heard till after broad day in the morning. I could frequently distinguish articulate sounds, and usually a shrill female voice would begin, and then two others with deeper and manlike tones seemed to join in the discourse, yet, though this conversation sounded as if close to me, I never could distinguish words."

At last, Mary Ricketts appealed to her brother, the Earl St. Vincent, to come to her aid. Earlier, he had spent a few days at Hinton Ampner and had heard nothing, but now the urgency in his sister's letter convinced him that whatever was troubling her was very real—at least to her and the servants.

When the Earl St. Vincent arrived at the mansion, he had in his company a well-armed man servant. The Earl was convinced that some disrespectful pranksters had conspired to annoy his sister and her household, and he was determined to deal out swift justice. He was joined in his campaign to "exorcise the spooks" by Captain Luttrell, a neighbor of the Ricketts. Captain Luttrell, who was familiar with the old legends of the area, had accepted the possibility of a supernatural agency at work, but he had volunteered his services to determine the cause of the disturbances, regardless of their origin.

The three armed men were kept on the go all night by the sound of doors opening and slamming. "Halt, who goes there?" Captain Luttrell shouted again and again at the plodding, heavy footsteps in the hallway. He never fired his pistol, because he was never offered a target. Finally he stopped shouting his command to halt. He began to feel a bit ridiculous—and more than a little frightened—by his attempts to get an invisible agency to obey him.

Mrs. Ricketts' brother had suddenly become a believer in the world unseen. He had soon concluded that the disturbances were definitely not the results of any human activity. Captain Luttrell declared that Hinton Ampner was unfit for human occupancy and urged Mrs. Ricketts to move out at once. The Earl St. Vincent agreed with his sister's neighbor, but he realized that she could not quit the house so easily. She needed a certain amount of time to notify her husband and the landlord of her decision, and the necessary preparations had to be made to obtain a different house.

"I'll stand guard every night for a week," he told Mary. "I'll sleep by day and watch by night."

The brother had maintained his vigil for about three nights when Mary was awakened by the sound of a pistol shot and the groans of a person in mortal agony. She was too frightened to move, but she felt secure in the knowledge that her brother and his servant were quite capable of handling any monster.

When her brother awakened the next afternoon, Mary quickly questioned him about the struggle that she heard the night before. The Earl St. Vincent frowned and shook his head in disbelief. He had heard no shot nor any of the terrible groaning.

The Earl himself was forced to experience the frustration of hearing sounds that no one else could perceive on the very next day. He was lying in his bed, having just awakened from his afternoon's sleep, when he heard an "immense weight that seemed to fall through the ceiling to the floor." He leaped out of bed, fully expecting to see a gaping hole in both ceiling and floor. There was not the slightest splinter, nor had anyone else in the mansion heard the crash. Even his servant, who slept in the bedroom directly below, had heard nothing.

The Earl insisted that his sister leave at once, and, because he was unable to stay at Hinton Ampner any longer, he ordered his Lieutenant of Marines to the mansion to assist Mary in her moving chores and to maintain the nightly watch.

Mrs. Ricketts gave notice to her landlord, Lady Hillsborough, and immediately set the servants to work packing trunks and bags. The night after her brother left, she and the entire household heard a crash such as the one that he had described. The crash was followed by several "piercing shrieks, dying away as though sinking into the earth."

"My, what a lovely sound that was," the nurse, Hannah Streeter, flippantly remarked. "I'd love to hear more like that."

Miss Streeter learned that one should never joke with a poltergeist. The unfortunate woman was troubled with horrid screaming and groaning in her room every night until the household moved away.

Mrs. Ricketts returned to Hinton Ampner only once after she had moved away. She entered the house alone and heard "a sound which I had never heard before ... a sound which caused me indescribable terror."

Lady Hillsborough sent her agent, a Mr. Sainsbury, to stay a night in the house and to test the truth of the rumors about her manor. Mr. Sainsbury did not last the night.

In 1772, a family named Lawrence moved into Hinton Ampner. Their servants reported seeing an apparition of a woman, but the Lawrences, for some reason, threatened their servants not to make any statements. They lasted a year before they moved out. After their occupancy, the house was pulled down to be used in the construction of a new manor.

When Mrs. Ricketts resided in the mansion, an old man had come to her with a tale about having boarded up a small container for Lord Stawell, the original owner of Hinton Ampner. He had suggested that the small box might have contained treasure and might offer a clue to the haunting. The container was discovered by workmen when they were stripping the mansion. It was found to conceal the skeleton of a baby.

When Mary Ricketts learned of this startling discovery, it seemed to offer the final key to the legend of Hinton Ampner. It had been rumored by the villagers that Lord Stawell had engaged in illicit relations with the younger sister of his wife, who had lived with them at the manor. It had been the subject of ancient gossip that his sister-in-law had borne his child—a child that had been murdered at its birth.

When Lady Stawell died, her sister, Honoria, became the mistress of Hinton Ampner. The past wrongs began to form a chain of evil. The first Lady Stawell, wronged by a younger sister and an indiscreet husband; the inno- cent babe, born of an illicit union, murdered, its body boarded up in the walls of the manor. Lord Stawell, the perpetrator of most of the sins, was himself left on his bed in the yellow room to die in agony, while his family waited without, ignoring his groans of pain.

It was shortly after Lord Stawell's death, in 1755,

that the groom swore that his old master had appeared to him in his room. The groom knew that it was the master because of the drab-colored gray clothing which Lord Stawell was so fond of wearing. From that time on, the "gray man" and his groans and plodding footsteps were heard in the corridors of Hinton Ampner. The "lady" was said to have been the phantom of the first Lady Stawell. Again it seems that old, bottled up memories of the dead had been activated by the frustrations and repressions of the living.

INVISIBLE FIREBUGS

THE POLTERGEIST had begun playing its unwelcome pranks in a more or less conventional manner during that summer of 1829. The John McDonalds, farmers near Baldoon, Ontario, had been jolted out of their sleep one night by what sounded like the heavy footsteps of many men stomping around in their kitchen. The startled farmer had searched the large frame house and the immediate grounds but had found nothing to account for the strange noises.

Throughout the summer, the night sounds of footsteps had continued to disturb their sleep. Mr. McDonald decreed to his household that they would ignore the noises and tell no one of their existence. He had set them a difficult task, but they—his wife, two sons, Allan and Neil, and 15-year-old Jane, a relative who had come to help with the new baby—complied with his wishes. By fall, however, the manifestations had become impossible to ignore. Streams of lead pellets had begun to bore through the glass windows, forcing McDonald to board up the openings.

Thirty persons witnessed the Rev. Alexander Brown pick up a bag full of pellets, mark them, and throw them in the river. Within moments, the objects were once again streaming in through the windows—dripping wet. Furniture became animated and the chairs moved about even while visitors were sitting on them! A hunter, who came to the door seeking shelter for the night, had his gun jerked from his hand and fired by the invisible entity. A visiting cobbler soon took his leave of the residence when the shoes that he had lined up for repair began to walk about the room by themselves.

All these disturbances the McDonald family had endured with admirable stoicism. It was when the poltergeist began to exhibit its incendiary abilities that the McDonalds felt that they had truly been cursed by a demon. The fireballs began to descend shortly after a Baptist preacher had conducted an abortive attempt at exorcism. In the midst of his prayer meeting, a huge stone had crashed through the front door and rolled across the farmhouse to rest at the feet of the preacher. It would be unfair, perhaps, to suggest that the hellfire preaching of the minister had actually stirred up the flames of Hades; but it wasn't long after his visit that the little puffs of fire were first seen, floating through the air, igniting any inflammable object on which they landed. As many as 50 outbreaks of fire a day were stamped out by the McDonalds and their neighbors.

McDonald ordered that no fires be lit in the house. "We'll have our meals brought over from father's home," he told his wife. "I don't even want you to light a fire for cooking. Maybe the thing feeds on fire, and we don't want to be giving it any fuel!"

Still the fires continued. Friends, neighbors, and members of the family were forced to keep a 24-hour firewatch. Buckets of water were scattered throughout the farmhouse and each of the outbuildings.

A schoolteacher made the mistake of enacting an ancient rite of "conjuring away an evil spirit" in the presence of the Constable and was arrested for practicing witchcraft. A Roman Catholic priest suggested to the farmer that he was being punished for some secret crime that the family had committed, and the indignant McDonald ordered the clergyman off the farm.

The McDonalds and their friends were kept continuously on the run, dousing the seemingly endless shower of fireballs. "Fires would even start on the wet floor," a witness of the extraordinary phenomena remembered. "Wet planking would burn as if it had been coated with oil. We had to keep drenching everything with water. We ran until we were nearly exhausted."

One morning, as the weary McDonalds ate a cold

breakfast, a fire managed to burst into a full flame without being noticed by any member of the family. The farmhouse burned as if it were dry tinder, and the McDonalds were unable to save a single piece of furniture or any of their personal possessions.

The same neighbors who had so unselfishly given of their time and energy to help the McDonalds in their attempt to ward off the fire demon, now offered to take the destitute family into their homes. But wherever the McDonalds went, the puffs of fire followed. The poltergeist had not faded after the climactic burning of the farmhouse. Its energy source was still active.

The McDonalds were forced to split up. The younger children and their mother went to stay with John McDonald's father. A brother-in-law offered to take in John and the others.

The poltergeist was only temporarily halted by this maneuver. Grandfather Daniel's farm was soon besieged by showers of lead pellets and stones. Worse, his farm animals began to sicken and die. John McDonald had taken to living in a tent to protect his brother-in-law's home, but even there he was visited by the greedy flames. Even wet clothing hung out on a line to dry would burst into flames.

The unseen firebug had now begun to launch an aerial attack against Daniel McDonald's farm, and once again farmhands and neighbors had to maintain a constant patrol against the machinations of the invisible incendiarist. One afternoon, a bundle of flaming sticks seemingly dropped from the sky to spread its destructive power to the barn roof. A number of men had seen the object fall and quickly handed buckets up to the flames on the roof. In spite of such vigilance, the granery with all of McDonald's harvested crops was completely destroyed. With winter coming on and their grain consumed by the persecuting flames, the McDonalds were left dependent on whatever food their neighbors could spare them.

The last days of the Baldoon poltergeist are confused ones, clouded with tales of witchcraft and a curse. An old neighbor woman received the accusations of being a witch, who had cursed the McDonalds for spite, and it is said that she was treated as an outcast until the day of her death. No one ever thought to associate the manifestations with Jane, the bright and pretty 15-year-old relative. But, of course, the McDonalds, their neighbors, and the villagers of Baldoon had never heard of a poltergeist, either. At any rate, much to the relief of everyone in Baldoon, the disturbances visited upon the McDonald family ceased one Sunday morning after church. John and his family, who had patched up their homestead, returned to find all their makeshift furniture piled in a heap. Their family Bible lay open, face down on the floor. The poltergeist had run out of psychic ammunition.

Is it possible that the human mind can, prism-like, focus enough raw energy to start fires? Is this strange power yet another unknown ability linked in some way to puberty? If so, can this power be perfected and practiced at will, in addition to being a manifestation of a fragmented psyche?

Vice-President Dawes encountered a most unusual Negro car repairman while visiting Memphis in 1927.

"This man had only to breathe upon objects to cause them to burst into flames," the astonished Vice-President said. "He cupped a handkerchief in his hands, breathed on it for a few seconds, then let it fall to the ground on fire."

In 1878, the farmers of Glasgow, Scotland were on the verge of burning 12-year-old Ann Kidner at the stake for witchcraft. Angry and disgruntled men testified that haystacks smoldered into flame at her very passing. One farmer claimed that his barn had burned to the ground after the young girl had made a "magical" gesture at it. Bewildered police officials arrested the girl, but young Ann was released upon her promise to stop doing whatever she had been doing.

Fourteen-year-old Jennie Bramwell of Toronto, Canada had the power of making objects burst into flame, simply by pointing her finger at them. Jennie, an orphan, was placed in a succession of foster homes with the same disasterous results—either the house or most of its furnishings would burn up.

A girl in Brooklyn at the turn of the century admitted being responsible for setting several houses on fire, including two which had sheltered her own family.

"It's true that I caused those fires," the 16-year-old girl confessed to police officials, "but I don't really know how."

"We've moved from town to town," her stepmother complained, "and everywhere it is the same terrible story. She's a wicked girl who sets fires to houses, barns, and stables."

The woman grabbed her stepdaughter by the shoulders and shook her until the girl began to cry. While she cursed and harrangued the sobbing teen-ager, the wallpaper of the room began to curl into flames under the very noses of the astounded police. It became suddenly apparent to the officers that somehow, in a way that they did not understand, the conflict between the girl and her stepmother was "igniting" the mysterious fires that had followed the unfortunate family.

POLTERGEISTS, PEBBLES, AND PHYSICS

WE ARE TOLD in the Bible that the Great Deluge flooded the world in forty days and forty nights. Imagine, if you can, the consternation of the family of Don Cid de Ulhoa Cento, who endured a stone-throwing poltergeist in their mansion in Sao Paulo, Brazil for the same length of time.

The paranormal bombardment began on Sunday, April 12, 1959. Don Cid was reading a paper while his wife, Dona Regina, and the maid, Francisca, were preparing lunch. The three children were playing in the front passageway.

Thud! Thud!

Don Cid put down his paper at the two loud raps. "What are the children getting into?" he called to his wife.

"I don't know," she called from the kitchen. "Will you go see?"

Don Cid frowned, annoyed at the interruption. He folded the paper and placed it on an end table next to his easy chair. It seemed as though one could not even enjoy a quiet Sunday without the children finding new ways of getting into trouble.

"Someone has thrown rocks in at us," Don Cid found his children whining in the front passage.

He bent and picked up two stones that lay on the floor. "Did you see someone throw them?" he asked the children.

The children shook their heads. "They just fell down beside us."

Don Cid scowled. Someone could have thrown the stones into the open passage from the courtyard. He looked out into the court but could see no one. Perhaps, he thought, a friend was playing a joke on them. He decided to go out into the courtyard to investigate further.

Senor Cento had only been outside a few moments when he heard cries coming from inside their large mansion. When he re-entered the house, he found stones falling in the passage, the kitchen, the pantry, the drawing room—every room in the house except the bedroom in which the two younger children had taken refuge.

Although his household was terrified, Don Cid remained strangely calm. With an almost detatched air, he tried to trace the trajectory of the missiles. He saw to it that all the doors and windows were securely fastened. He carefully examined the ceiling and the walls for holes.

By now, the stones were not only falling, but they had begun to hit the walls and roll about on the floor as if they possessed a life of their own. Some were even leaping into the air like Mexican jumping beans.

Senor Cento clutched a few in his hands and found them to be warm to the touch. He continued to pursue the falling, rolling, jumping rocks for two hours before he decided to call in some neighbors. The friends who gathered at the Cento mansion were of no help in coming up with a rational explanation for the extraordinary bombardment. All they were able to do was to stand stupefied as the stones continued to rain down on the hapless Cento family.

Don Cid was a devout Roman Catholic. He endured the phenomena for two days, then he decided that it was time to call in a priest to bless the house. The Rev. Father Henrique de Morais Matos, vicar of the parish, answered the summons. Although the disturbances had added flying peppers, kitchen utensils, and pots to its artillery, the priest seemed more fascinated than frightened by the manifestations. He, too, was calm enough to concern himself with trajectory and direction, and he even conducted an experiment with the ambitious poltergeist.

Observing an egg floating through the air, the Father snatched it up and placed it in the refrigerator. After a few moments, he noticed an egg strike a wall in the pantry. He picked it up. It was cold. He ran to the refrigerator, opened it, and found that the egg that he had placed there was no longer on the shelf where he had lain it.

Father Matos performed the rites of exorcism and the phenomena ceased. The period proved to be a truce rather than a defeat for the poltergeist, however. Eleven days later, the rooms in the Centos' mansion were once again raining rocks. Exorcism was repeated twice more with the same temporary benefits.

Francisca, the 22-year-old maid, had immediately come under suspicion by her employer as somehow being responsible for the activity. He kept her under close surveillance and soon had to admit that "she was not guilty of trickery or of causing the disturbance by any natural means."

Spiritualists, however, insisted that the young maid possessed great mediumistic powers of which she was unaware. Prankish spirits had been attracted to Francisca, the spiritualists declared, and they were causing the fall of stones and other objects in Don Cid's home.

Newspaper reporters could not help noticing that Francisca, a simple, uneducated maid, remained completely calm throughout the most violent demonstrations. One reporter observed large stones that fell in succession, narrowly missing the maid. She seemed not to display the least concern for her safety, but continued to go about her work in the kitchen.

The stone-throwing at the town of Itapura in the state of Sao Paulo, Brazil is among the best attested in modern times. The phenomena was witnessed by a police inspector, an attorney general, a priest, several physicians, a number of school teachers, and, of course, numerous journalists.

Ivan T. Sanderson, world-famous zoologist, natural historian, and investigator of the unusual, insists that one should not use the term "throwing" when speaking of the poltergeistic manipulation of stones. "The stones are not thrown; they are *dropped* or lobbed or just drift around," Sanderson maintains.

Sanderson goes on to declare that such cases are within the realm of physics rather than parapsychology. Stone-dropping is "purely physical phenomena," according to Sanderson, and can, in time, be "completely explained on some physical principles, though not necessarily on Newtonian, Einsteinian, or any others that concern our particular space-time continuum."

Sanderson, who once "played catch" with flying rocks in Sumatra, feels that "if somebody would measure their speed of fall on arrival, it might be demonstrated that they are obeying some law or, at least, following some pattern that is not entirely random . . . they might be obeying some other so-called 'law' of dynamics. If we could establish this, we would have at least two principles of dynamics in our space-time continuum."

THE STONE-THROWING DEVIL

A STRONG CASE could probably be made for the assertion that the famous Salem witchcraft hysteria is an example of poltergeistic phenomena that got out of hand. The young girls, who claimed to have been bewitched by various old crones in the village, complained of being pinched, having their hair pulled, and being stuck with pins. All these symptoms of a witch's wickedness we now recognize as familiar manifestations of the poltergeist.

Pursuing this thesis for just a bit longer, we might observe that throughout the centuries witches have traditionally been given the power to command invisible agents to hurl stones at their victims, and the awesome talent of being able to torment people by the production of eerie night noises and destructive fires. All of these powers of the witch coincide with attributes of the poltergeist. Perhaps an accomplished witch is simply one who has somehow learned to control and to retain that strange fragmentation of the psyche which sometimes occurs during pubertal change.

Such would seem to be the case in the disturbances which beset the George Walton family in 1662. Walton, an ambitious farmer who lusted for more land, had eyed the few acres that bordered his farm with an ever-growing greed. The bit of land was owned by an elderly widow, who lived in a small cabin on the acreage. Walton knew that she had neither money nor influential friends, so he had her charged with witchcraft. Then, either through legal chicanery or the greasing of the proper official palms, the greedy farmer obtained her land, which had been confiscated by the authorities.

"You'll never quietly enjoy that ground," the widow cursed him.

Walton merely laughed at the old woman's malediction, but he did have the decency to drop his charges of witchcraft against the poor, now homeless widow.

On a Sunday night shortly after Walton had moved his family into the widow's house there came a fierce bombardment of stones against the roof and doors.

"Indians!" Walton shouted, reaching for his musket. The occupants of the house cautiously looked out into moonlit fields and saw nothing. No one.

Then, as they blinked unbelieving eyes, the front gate was wrenched from its hinges by invisible hands and tossed high into the air.

Walton ventured out to investigate, his musket clenched firmly in his hands. A volley of stones was suddenly hurled at him, and he fled back into the cabin.

"Bar the doors and windows!" he puffed as he slammed the front door behind him. His family quickly obeyed, but shutters made no difference to the stones. In they came, through glass, through shutter, rolling down the chimney, smashing against the door.

Objects in the room began to hurl themselves at George Walton. Candles were blown out. The bars on the doors began to bend under the solid blows of an invisible hammer. A cheese-press smashed itself against a wall.

Somehow, the Waltons managed to survive that

night of horror. The devil had not vanished with the coming of dawn and the cock's crowing, however. That day, haystacks in the fields were broken up and the hay tossed into the high branches of trees. As Walton attempted to go about his farm labors, the stones pursued him.

Richard Chamberlayne, secretary to the Governor of New Hampshire, who later wrote a pamphlet on the "Diabolick Inventions of the Devil," lived with the Waltons during the three-month span of the violent disturbances. He tried desperately to trace the source of the pelting stones and at first suggested that the activity might be the work of "naughty little boys." Chamberlayne had no sooner spoke these words, he writes, than one of the boys, who had been helping the workmen put up hay, was struck so hard on the back that he began to cry.

The Waltons' "devil" never developed a voice, but it was quite proficient at snorting and whistling. And, although it kept up a steady barrage of stones, it was never too busy to smash pottery and slam furniture about the room.

Even if one feels that the greedy Walton deserved to have a "devil" set on him after he had displaced the poor widow and taken her land, one has to admire the perserverence of the man, who kept right at his farm work in spite of the vicious personal attacks of the stone-thrower.

Chamberlayne declares that Walton often received more than forty "shrewd, hurtful blows" in a single day. Several rows of corn were uprooted "as if by a sharp tool." His hired men had sickle blades broken by the stones as the tools were knocked out of their hands by the invisible demon. Chamberlayne himself once received a "smart blow on the leg."

After about three months, the bombardment of stones ceased. In 1662, of course, the entire disturbance was immediately accredited to the curse of a witch. To have thought otherwise would have been heresy. And, as we have already noted, perhaps some people do have the power to activate poltergeistic manifestations by the intense exertion of negative psychic suggestion.

THE PHANTOM MARKSMAN OF KOKOMO

CAPTAIN OF DETECTIVES C. C. Unger set down the receiver of the telephone with an air of exasperated disbelief. "That's the twentieth complaint I've taken this morning about bullet holes in a store window," he said to a patrolman. "After that quiet weekend, we suddenly have a nut with an air gun running loose in Kokomo!"

By Thursday of the week of September 22, 1952, fifty businessmen had complained that someone was shooting holes in their plate glass windows. The perforations were all similar—a small opening through the glass, too small to have come from a B-B shot or an air gun pellet, with a crater smashed on the inside of the glass at the point of impact. The damaged area was about the size of a quarter, and most were at eye level or a bit above.

As it was apparent that the holes had all been made by the same type of missile, Captain Unger began conducting his investigation on the premise that someone had set about shooting up the business district with an air rifle. He conducted thorough tests with all types of air rifles in an attempt to come up with the gun that was responsible for the damage. But no make of air rifle available to Captain Unger had caused the holes. The methodical police official simply could not approximate the peculiar perforations in the crime lab.

Police Chief Don Scott issued a front page appeal in the Kokomo *Tribune,* asking anyone who had any information which might offer a clue to the steadily rising damage to downtown Kokomo, to step forward and declare himself. No citizen contacted Chief Scott. They were all as baffled as the police.

Captain Unger was becoming increasingly frustrated as complaints about the phantom sharpshooter continued to come into the police department. The area of the destruction bothered him. Hw could anyone with a rifle, even if it were some noiseless type of air gun, roam about a downtown business district shooting store windows, without attracting any witnesses? It seemed impossible that anyone could travel over central Kokomo for a total of approximately 60 blocks, shooting 50 or more holes in plate glass windows without being observed by a single citizen.

Another eerie facet to the case, Captain Unger reported to the Chief, was that not a single pellet or shot was ever found. How could anyone shoot holes in windows without leaving a pellet *somewhere* on the inside of the glass? This, plus the fact that Captain Unger had found it impossible to match the holes with any identified type of gun, forced the police to abandon the notion of a mad marksman wandering the streets of Kokomo.

But what theory did the police substitute? If the holes were not caused by a man with a gun, who or what did cause them? To complicate the case, Peru, Indiana, a city 21 miles north of Kokomo, had received a brief visit from the phantom marksman in the middle of that same week. Obviously the invisible sharpshooter had found the targets more to his liking in Kokomo, for only six windows had been punctured in Peru.

Because of the large amount of damage done to the glass in the downtown district, the Kokomo police conducted an exhaustive investigation in an attempt to apprehend the guilty parties. Not a single lead was ever uncovered, nor was anyone ever arrested. Today, the case of the Phantom Marksman is listed as one of the few unsolved crimes on the Kokomo police blotter.

WHO THREW THOSE ROCKS?

"IT IS MY considered opinion that you are being dive-bombed by sea gulls which have obtained rocks from the beach."

Mrs. Irene Fellows could only stare unbelievingly at the so-called investigator who had just offered an opinion even more fantastic than the disturbances that she and her grandchildren had been enduring. For two weeks, Mrs. Fellows, Donna Lee Wade, five, and Audrey, nine, had been bruised by stones that seemed to fall from nowhere.

The Oakland, California police had been frankly skeptical when they had received her frantic call on August 17, 1943. Mrs. Fellows had claimed that someone was pelting her stucco home on 89th Avenue with stones.

When two bemused patrolmen arrived to investigate the complaint, they were quick to notice that the walls and roof of the cottage were unmistakably pockmarked from the impact of falling rocks. Their amusement quickly turned to professional concern as they examined the indentations. Then, as they questioned the frightened woman, a stone fall occurred, hammering the roof with violent intensity.

"It has been like this since dawn," Mrs. Fellows insisted.

The policeman looked outside, and even the trained skeptics could not ignore the many piles of worn rocks that littered the lawn.

An official vigil began on August 18th. The police officers interviewed the neighbors—with special emphasis on the children—and exonerated all of them. Whatever was responsible for hurling the rocks seemed to react against the interference of the police by launching malicious attacks on Mrs. Fellows and her grandchildren. Several witnesses saw the inhabitants of the stucco cottage receive barrages of stones that struck and bruised their bodies. Grandma Fellows was dealt a solid blow on the shoulder even as she talked with Sergeant Austin Page.

Sightseers began to arrive, and some of them boldly invaded the lawn to collect the "bewitched" stones as curios. Someone suggested that Mrs. Fellows open a museum to display her "stones from the blue."

Scientists from the nearby University of California investigated Oakland's mystery house and acknowledged these brief facts: whenever Mrs. Fellows and her grandchildren left their home, stones from a cloudless sky struck one or more of them. Other stones fell on the cottage. No stones were visible until they hit. The stones made no sound in flight. They came from all directions and fell with sufficient force to mark the house or bruise the bodies of Mrs. Fellows, Donna Lee, and Audrey.

At noon, September 1, Mrs. Fellows, sleepless and exhausted, was talking with Special Officers Johnston and Nordendahl, in her garden. The stones had been falling day and night for two weeks, and the elderly woman was on the brink of a nervous collapse. As the three of them were trying to chat about something other than dropping rocks, a huge stone suddenly crashed onto the roof of the cottage and tumbled down at their feet. It was the last mysterious rock to pelt the stucco cottage on 89th Avenue.

POLTERGEIST OF THE ANDES

THE INDIAN WAS in a state of high excitement when he entered the village of Jauja and sought out Father Conde.

"Please, Father," the Indian begged. "You must return home with me and drive out the devils that have taken possession of our house!"

Father Conde managed to calm the Indian, whose name was Vasquez, and gain the particulars concerning the desperate request for exorcism. It seemed that the members of his family had been set upon by a stone-throwing devil that had beleagured them for over a week. Sometimes the devil threw stones at them during the day, but especially at night when the doors were closed and the shutters firmly bolted.

The priest was convinced that something was bothering the Indian and his family. The man was known to him, and he was a simple man of truth, not given to wild storytelling. Father Conde enlisted the company of the mayor and an American mining engineer, and the three of them set out for the Indian's adobe hut.

There was nothing unusual about the appearance of the haunted home as they approached it from the dusty path. It was the typical one-story affair of adobe brick, roofed with rough native tile. The house proper was a combined living room and kitchen, a bedroom and a storeroom.

Vasquez's wife was hysterical. Her face and head were covered with bumps and scars. His three girls, aged eight to fifteen, had fared no better. They, too, looked as though they had been pelted half to death. Vasquez showed his visitors a pile of rocks, ranging in size from pebbles to cobblestones and including lumps of dried mud and pieces of broken tile.

"All these," the Indian sighed, "have been thrown at my family during the past ten days."

"And what of yourself?" the priest asked him.

The Indian shrugged, his palms turned upward. "For some reason, the devil has never struck me."

The American mining engineer frowned. "Well, your family has certainly been taking a beating from something—or someone," he said, narrowing his eyes suspiciously at Vasquez.

If the Indian was aware of the American's suspicions, he did not seem to be bothered by them. Vasquez knew that he was not guilty of mistreating his family. If the men stayed in the hut for a while, they would soon see that it was a devil that was abusing his wife and daughters.

The priest and the mayor had been carefully inspecting the interior of the Vasquez home. Several walls bore deep indentations that could only have been made by hard objects thrown against them. Pottery, earthenware, and holy pictures had been smashed.

"The devil does not bother my family if they leave the house," Vasquez explained, "but the moment they enter the hut, he begins to throw stones at them."

The priest persuaded one of the girls, an intelligent-looking child of about twelve, to sit in a chair in the center of the storeroom. The girl's head and face were badly bruised and cut, but she did as she was asked.

The American engineer closed the heavy wooden door leading to the living room, and the three men—the engineer, Father Conde, and the mayor—stood shoulder to shoulder in the doorway, their backs against the door. The girl sat facing them in the center of the room. Suddenly a large stone struck the girl's cheek with enough force to jerk her sideways. With difficulty, she remained seated on the chair, but she could not control the sobs of pain that shook her frail body.

The mayor ran forward and scooped up the stone. "This cannot be!" he shouted.

The three men kept the door closed and searched the walls of the storeroom inch by inch. The ceiling and walls were of hard mud. There was no place where anyone could have been concealed.

The girl had been hit on the cheek, so the rock had

to have come from one side of the room. The engineer determined that from the sound of the thud and the effect of the blow, it gave evidence of having been thrown underhanded from a distance of about six feet. But there was no one in the room who could have thrown the stone. And none of them had seen the stone in flight. One minute the girl was sitting there in the middle of the room, smiling pleasantly at them. The next, she had been struck a cruel blow on the cheek with a large rock.

The girl's face was beginning to swell, so the men returned her to her mother, who did what she could for her. The American engineer displayed both the frustration of a practical man confronted by the impossible, and a Yankee's eagerness to do at least some small thing to help someone in need. He went back to the village and bought some beer for the parents and some beaded necklaces for the girls. At least the native beer and the trinkets could alleviate the suffering inflicted upon the family by that "invisible devil of the Andes."

Father Conde performed the rites of exorcism, but the stones continued to pelt the females of the Vasquez family for another week before the phenomenon stopped as suddenly as it had begun.

A SPOOK MAKES A HOUSE AWFULLY CROWDED

THE *Des Moines Register* called the valleys of Millville, Iowa "an ideal haunt for a noisy ghost." The newspaper described the "ghost house" as being "at the dead end of a branch off Split Level Road where black crows abound in a creek valley and outcroppings of rock jut forth like spectres."

It was on Thanksgiving evening, 1959, that the headline provoking disturbances began in the William Meyer home. Meyer, an alert 83-year-old, was bed-ridden with a broken hip and was taking his ease in a corner of the living room that had been converted into a bedroom for the duration of his convalescence. His wife was resting in an easy chair across the room. His grandson, Gene Meyer, was sitting on the edge of the bed. As was their habit, the lights were off while they were resting.

Suddenly a loud noise sounded above them, startling them and throwing them into momentary confusion. When the lights were turned on, Gene's face was covered with a black, dust-like substance, and the mysterious stuff settled over much of the room.

Elmer Meyer, the Meyer's son who lived on the next farm, was summoned to see the substance that he later described as "wet and gray like soot." His mother was in the process of sweeping the mess up, and she was able to fill two dustpans with the "real fine dirt" before she had tidied up the room.

All the Meyers were baffled by the sudden appearance of the soot-like substance. The woodburning stove had not exploded. The walls and ceiling were solid and airtight, and the stovepipe had no visible cracks or holes.

For the next few days, the Meyers joked and talked freely about the "black face" Gene had received, and discussed the mystery good-naturedly with their friends and neighbors.

On December 16th, the strange event had ceased to be a matter for joking. As their 16-year-old grandson once again sat with them in their darkened living room, the Meyers were startled to hear another loud thud. When the lights were turned on, they discovered that a wooden flower stand had fallen over and that a plate filled with Christmas cards, which had been resting on top of the pedestal, had slid across the room to rest beneath Meyer's bed.

While the three Meyers puzzled over this disturbance, Mrs. Meyers was doused with a glass of water, which she claimed she saw rise in the air before it struck her.

Again Elmer Meyer, Gene's father, was called to the home of his parents. A practical-minded farmer, Elmer concluded that the house must be undergoing a series of vibrations from some natural source. To test his theory, he placed a fresh egg on the top of a lamp chimney and instructed everyone to watch it to see if there would be any movement.

Elmer maintained his vigil for over two hours before he left his parents' home. After he had gone, Gene said: "Everything else has happened in the dark. Maybe if

93

we turn out the lights, things will start happening again."

The lights were turned off, and the three Meyers once again sat in the dark, waiting to see if the "vibrations" would act up. They had not sat long before they heard a series of loud "splats." When the lights were turned back on, the egg was found smashed against the door, and several chunks of mud were discovered on the wall above Grandpa Meyer's bed.

Although they were considerably upset, the Meyers decided not to call their son again that night. They cleaned up the mess and went to bed, leaving Gene to go home to inform his father of the weird happenings that had taken place after his departure.

The next day, the disturbances became impossible for the elderly man and woman to tolerate. Toward dark, they were alarmed by what sounded like "nine or ten men upstairs knocking boards off the roof." These noises continued for about twenty minutes. Mrs. Meyers had just got up enough courage to begin the evening meal's dishes when there was a loud smashing sound in the milk pantry. Cautiously investigating, she found that an old refrigerator, which was used to store empty jars and bottles, had fallen to the floor. As it tipped to the floor, it had knocked down a table of dishes and some of the milk separating equipment. For the first time in the sequence of disturbances, their teen-aged grandson was not present. He had been on the road, walking to pick up the day's mail when the dramatic events took place. Elmer Meyer, the boy's father, later substantiated Gene's whereabouts, when he stated that he had seen his son on the road at the time of the disturbances on the roof and in the milk pantry.

The elderly couple had had enough "spook" business. They called an ambulance and asked to be taken into the nearby village of Guttenberg so that they might stay with relatives. William Meyer later explained his abrupt departure to investigators Arthur Hastings and Stanley Krippner by telling them: "I didn't know what would have happened next; if I stayed, I would probably be dead by now."

Mrs. Fred Meyer of Guttenberg told reporters: "We don't want them to go back until we know what's happening down there. The whole house might be swallowed up—that's limestone country, you know, and there's springs—water might have opened up a hole under the house."

Elmer was, at this time, sticking to his theory of "vibrations." He pointed out that "there's a spring on one side of the house, and a creek runs by the other. That might cause some of these things somehow, some way."

On New Year's Day, Elmer Meyer asked Clayton County Sheriff Forrest M. Fischer to accompany him on an investigation of the vacated house. Shortly after his parents had moved, Elmer had shown a photographer through the farmhouse. As they had entered the basement, a large rock had dislodged itself from a wall and had smashed a ten-gallon crock. "That didn't have to happen," Meyer had remarked to the photographer in taciturn understatement.

Sheriff Fischer bluntly told Meyer that he thought the whole business to be a bunch of "hocus-pocus," but he agreed to begin a more thorough investigation of the disturbances.

As Meyer, Sheriff Fischer, and three reporters walked through the house on New Year's Day, a newsman saw a bottle jump out of a packing case and smash itself on the floor. The reporters spent a few confused moments accusing one another of dropping the bottle, but all denied personal responsibility.

On Wednesday, January 6th, a group of Elmer Meyer's friends declared that they would spend the night in the haunted house. Among the farmer's friends was a burly, 265-pound Great Lakes ship pilot named Pat Livingston, who became personally involved in the most spectacular of the phenomena, when he was tossed out of bed by the "ghost."

"I am a first-rate pilot," Livingston told reporters. "I'm no crackpot. I don't believe it, but it happened."

Livingston had gone to bed that night while his companions continued to sit up in the kitchen. It was about ten o'clock when the husky pilot saw the chair beside the bed begin to move.

"The thing bobbled across the floor for about eight feet and tipped over," he said. "I thought maybe some of the other people had tied a string on it and pulled it away, but they denied it."

Livingston had only been back in bed for a few seconds when ". . . the next thing I knew, I was lying on the floor. I'll take a lie detector test or anything. I woke up kind of groggy. I wouldn't have believed it for love or money."

The big man insisted that nothing human had moved him and the mattress off the bed. "None of the people present were big enough to do it," Livingston explained. "And when anyone grabs me, I grab back!"

Gene Meyer, who was in the house the night that the burly ship's pilot was dumped out of bed, told reporters: "Pat was going to make a big joke out of it. He was the most surprised man I've ever seen."

Investigators Hastings and Krippner later suggested that the beers that Livingston had downed may have had something to do with his being bounced out of bed. Krippner remarked that the "spirits were not in the bed but in the sailor."

By now, the story of strange goings-on at the Meyer farmhouse had attracted nationwide attention. Wire-services had picked up the reports, radio and television stations were giving it a big play, and *Newsweek* magazine had considered it noteworthy enough to be listed in its compilation of weekly news items. Accounts became garbled and exaggerated. One newspaper spoke of "chairs, beds, and refrigerators tipping over spontaneously, dishes, glassware, and eggs leaping around the room, and mysterious noises which leave a coating of dust in their wake."

Students, professors, and scientists from nearby colleges and universities began descending upon the eerie farm country. Ion counters, oscilloscopes, Geiger counters, and argon radiation counters were set up in the deserted farmhouse. Teams of students and professors maintained 'round-the-clock vigils as they sought to trap a spook in their electronic nets.

A physics professor noted that the ion counter had "registered a high negative reading when we first came into the room, which is unusual, but after the air had circulated a little, the readings were quite normal."

The Geiger counter, it was reported, indicated only

"normal residual radiation." The argon radiation counters discovered no crack or fault in the bedrock. The oscilloscope registered only a normal 60-cycle sine wave "picked up from the house wiring."

State University of Iowa students reported no weird noises during the night except "that guy's snoring downstairs."

By the time that researchers Hastings and Krippner arrived on the scene, the only active disturbances were emanating from the unruly crowd of curiosity seekers who gathered outside the farmhouse at night.

Ralph Ingerson, a staff writer for the Dubuque *Telegraph Herald,* wrote of a night inside the ghost house that kept the "insiders" busy combatting the "outsiders" who wanted to investigate the spooks at first hand. The spectators became an ugly mob when Elmer Meyer denied them entrance into the farmhouse. "We never wreck nothin'," someone in the mob shouted. "We just came to look. Let us take a look! That's what we pay taxes for!"

The mob began to pound on the door until it reached a point where it seemed the door might cave in. At this moment, the "insiders" opened the door and fired flashguns into the dark, temporarily blinding the "outsiders." Another group smashed in the basement door and began to pour into the house until they, too, were driven back by the flash guns. Finally, reports that the sheriff was on his way sent the rowdy elements tearing off with a loud roar of mufflers.

After conducting extensive interviews with the participants in the poltergeist phenomena of the Millville farmhouse, investigators Hastings and Krippner felt that the majority of the disturbances could be attributed to psychological expectancy set, misinterpretation of natural mishaps, and impulse behavior on the part of human agents. Although the investigators did not rule out the possibility of psychic causes being responsible for some of the strange events, Hastings and Krippner suggested that the agency behind most of the manifestations was mortal rather than ghostly.

The investigators developed their theory more completely in an article entitled "Expectancy Set and 'Poltergeist' Phenomena," which appeared in volume XVIII, No. 3 of *Etc.: A Review of General Semantics.*

"Set," Hastings and Krippner explain, "may make us expect certain general or specific events. It may get us ready for particular actions, for particular thought processes, or to organize incoming material in particular ways. Set is based on our past experience and our present personality structure—our needs, emotions, attitudes and values . . . it [set] may make us misinterpret events in the world about us.

". . . a natural, but rare, event might demand explanation. If an easy explanation is not found, talk may turn to 'spooks.' Once this theory is accepted, or even seriously discussed, later events may be interpreted in this light and reinforce this theory."

Hastings and Krippner feel that expectancy set, a ghost of the mind, can cause people to misevaluate, to distort, and to misperceive events. Once a "set" becomes the pervading interpretation of a situation, a correct evaluation can never be made from the facts available.

To illustrate the power of expectancy set on the human mind, Hastings and Krippner, in their article, invite the reader to try an experiment with himself as the guinea pig. "The next time your house or apartment is free of guests or family, and when you return home late at night (alone), let yourself imagine that you left the door unlocked. Imagine that a dangerous criminal has been reported in the vicinity. If these conditions can be imagined, things will be noticed that would never have been apparent otherwise. A magazine will be out of place; a drawer will be open. The sofa will have a dent in its cushion as if it had recently been occupied. The longer you listen and the greater your expectancy set, the more varied noises you will be able to hear."

"POPPER" MOVES TO LONG ISLAND

THERE CAN'T HAVE been many children who have been welcomed home from school by a five-gun salute, but when the Herrmann children, thirteen-year-old Lucille and twelve-year-old James, Jr., walked in their front door at three-thirty on the afternoon of February 3, 1958, the caps of bottles located in various rooms of their suburban Long Island home began to pop like champagne corks.

Scurrying from room to room, Mrs. Lucille Herrmann and her two children found that a bottle of bleaching fluid had blown its top in the basement. In the kitchen, they located an uncapped bottle of liquid starch. The bathroom yielded both an uncapped bottle of shampoo and a topless bottle of liquid medicine. Mrs. Herrmann also discovered that a bottle of holy water had been spilled in the master bedroom.

Mrs. Herrmann called her husband, who was a representative for Air France in New York City, and reported the strange "poppings" that had sounded in their house. Herrmann was puzzled, but since no one had been hurt by the "explosions," he decided that he would not come home any earlier than he was accustomed.

James Herrmann arrived home with a solution already fixed in his mind. Some chemical reaction in the formulas of the various products had caused them to erupt. The fact that the bottles had all popped at once was undoubtedly due to some weird coincidence and probably had resulted from excessive humidity or some such thing in the house. He was a bit baffled, however, when he noted that each of the bottles had screw caps, which required several turns before they could be removed. If the bottles had had the crimped caps commonly used on soda pop bottles, his theory would have seemed much more valid. It seemed quite impossible that a chemical reaction could have blown off the screw caps without taking along the bottles' necks as well. He was relieved when his family gave every indication of having calmed down and no longer seemed to demand an explanation of him.

There were no further disturbances in the Herrmann household until two days later. Then it was a repeat performance of the poltergeist's debut. The children walked in the front door from school and the "fireworks" began. A bottle of nail polish popped open, and so did a bottle of rubbing alcohol, a bottle of bleach, starch, detergent, and the holy water. Once again, all the caps were of the screw-on variety.

When the bottles began to pop on the next night as

well, James Herrmann began to suspect that his science-fiction loving son had somehow hatched a little plot whereby he might have some fun at the expense of his family. Herrmann conjectured that James, Jr. could have dropped some type of carbonate capsule into the bottles and loosened their lids in the morning before he left for school. The boy was clever. He had probably succeeded in timing the "explosions" so that he could be present to witness the startled expression on the face of his mother.

Herrmann spent most of that weekend in surreptitious observance of his son. He was determined to catch the boy in some action that would give him away as the agent behind the mysterious poppings. No one, therefore, could have been more surprised than Herrmann when, on Sunday morning, several bottle caps popped off the holy water, the starch, and the turpentine, and their containers began to jiggle on the shelves. He had kept an eye on the boy day and night. How could he have slipped anything into the bottles?

James Jr. stood at the bathroom sink and vigorously proclaimed his innocence. He had been brushing his teeth when his father had burst into the room and began to interrogate him. As Herrmann questioned his son, he was startled to see a medicine bottle move across the sink top and smash itself to the floor. Within seconds, it was joined by a bottle of shampoo.

"This is too much," James Herrmann declared. "We've got troubles!"

He got on the phone and called the police, begging the officer who answered to take him seriously. Yes, that was correct. They were being bothered by bottles that popped their caps and flew about the room. The officer accused Herrmann of drinking, but he agreed to send a policeman to investigate the disturbances. James Herrmann had a good reputation in the community. It wasn't like him to annoy the police with such wild stories.

Patrolman James Hughes arrived at the Hermann residence sadly wondering why it was always he who seemed to draw all the odd-ball cases. He had only been in the house a few minutes, however, before several bottles in the bathroom fired a barrage at him. He rapidly concluded that the Herrmanns did, indeed, have "troubles."

Detective Joseph Tozzi listened to Patrolman Hughes' report with professional interest. He had not yet seen or heard the phenomena, so he could still be coldly dispassionate and objective about such things as popping bottle caps and flying objects.

"If bottles are acting up at the Herrmanns," he said, "they're doing it with human help. If the Herrmanns aren't guilty of trickery, then they're suffering from hallucinations. Or maybe some natural force, like radio waves are to blame. I don't know what's causing the trouble yet, but I do know that bottles can't fly by themselves."

Detective Tozzi began his vigil on February 11th. On that day, an atomizer in the teen-aged daughter's room tipped over when no one was in her bedroom. Or, Detective Tozzi noted skeptically, at least no one claimed to have been in the bedroom.

For the next few days, the disturbances were confined to bothering the bottle of holy water in the parents' bedroom. On the evening of February 15th, however, the manifestations of the poltergeist's powers became much more impressive. As the family sat watching television, a porcelain figurine lifted itself from a coffee table and began to float through the air.

After this demonstration of prowess on the part of their uninvited guest, the Herrmanns decided to call upon a man of the Cloth to aid the baffled Detective Tozzi in his investigations. Father William McLeod of the Church of Saint William the Abbott answered their plea for clerical help and administered a blessing to the home by sprinkling holy water liberally in six rooms. But the priest was too late. "Popper," as the strange force in the Herrmann house had come to be called, had grown too strong to have his spark of psychic life extinguished by holy water.

Much worse than the antics of Popper, the Herrmanns soon discovered, was the invasion of privacy that had occurred when the news media began to give their strange house a great deal of publicity. Letters in barely intelligible scrawls arrived, either condemning them for heinous sins or encouraging them to take heart and hold

101

fast against the evil tricks of Satan. Self-appointed ministers of various "gospels" began to conduct rituals on their front lawn.

One letter sympathized with the Herrmanns and informed them that he, too, had been afflicted with moving furniture. In this case, the agency responsible had been a fireplace with a heavy downdraft. Detective Tozzi agreed that capping the chimney with a rotary metal turbine might be a possible solution to the bizarre occurrences, and Herrmann had one installed.

The workmen had no sooner completed the installation when a porcelain figurine flew off a table top to smash against a desk. The figurine had managed a flight of over twelve feet! Seventeen days after its arrival, Popper was steadily acquiring the strength to perform more dramatic and more spectacular demonstrations. On February 20th, another figurine became airborne; a bottle of ink unscrewed its cap and splashed its contents against a wall; a sugar bowl took its leave of the dining table.

The Herrmanns, who had remained remarkably calm and patient throughout the phenomena, decided that they needed to get away from the house before their nerves gave out. While they spent the night of February 21st with relatives, Detective Tozzi maintained his vigil in the house that Popper had taken over with its infantile pranks. Although Tozzi's attitude toward paranormal manifestations had altered considerably from the first night that he had spent with the Herrmanns, it didn't bother him in the least to remain alone in the "haunted house." The night was quiet and without incident. There were no "poppings," no moving of furniture, no flying figurines. It would seem that the energy center was one of the pubertal children in the Herrmann family—or perhaps both of them. Both children strenuously professed their innocence of any trickery and, consciously, they may have been guiltless. Just as the poltergeist may be unaware that it is dependent on a living personality, as in the case of the Bell Witch, so may the energy center for the phenomena be completely ignorant of his role in the disturbance.

The truce at the Herrmann house was ended on the night that the family returned. Once again the sugar-bowl became so animated that it shot off the table and crashed to the floor.

On February 24th, Detective Tozzi was sent to his feet by the sound of a loud thud that had come from James, Jr.'s room. He was certain that no one had been in the room or near it, but upon entering the bedroom, he found that a heavy bureau had been tipped face down on the floor.

The next night, the boy's phonograph orbited itself around the room while he was doing his homework. In the master bedroom, a statuette of the Virgin Mary flew over twelve feet to strike the frame of a mirror across the room. A bookcase full of bulky encyclopedias was up-ended. A globe of the world shot down a hall-way, narrowly missing Detective Tozzi. A photographer saw his own flashbulbs raise themselves from a table, float across the room, and bounce against a wall. For the first time, Popper began to knock on the wall, but no attempt at any sort of "communication" was made.

Detective Tozzi was worried about the sudden flurry of violent activity on the part of Popper. He had had the place checked by electricians, physicists, and even by the Air Force to determine whether or not jet flight patterns might somehow be causing supersonic vibrations. He had taken the advice of occultists, self-styled preachers, anonymous letter-writers—any plan that had seemed remotely plausible, he had tried to apply to the Herrmann household. But nothing had worked. The manifestations seemed to be definitely growing in strength and were becoming increasingly violent in their demonstrations. Just as the detective was about to recommend that the family move to avoid personal harm, it seemed as though Popper suddenly used up its last reserves of energy during the recent flurry of activity.

The poltergeist said its "goodbye" at ten o'clock on the evening of March 2nd. It sent a dish shattering in the dining room, a night table falling in James Jr.'s bedroom, and a bookcase tumbling in the basement. With this parting gesture, Popper seemed to deteriorate into the oblivion reserved for fragmented psyches.

THE UNINVITED LODGER

MRS. CHARLES DAUGHTREY, who is "about a hundred years old, give or take a few years," was grumbling about the bad habit her 13-year-old grandson had of leaving his bed unmade in the morning.

"You'd think that boy could get up early enough in the morning to make his own bed," she said to herself as she finished tucking the sheets in under the mattress. "There," she sighed, "that's that."

Mrs. Daughtrey had no sooner stepped back to smooth the bedspread when the covers, mattress, and pillow all came flying up at her.

On that September Thursday in 1962, the bounding bed-clothes were but the first of a series of eerie phenomena that moved in with the Charles Daughtreys at 949 Florida Avenue, Portsmouth, Virginia. Mr. and Mrs. Daughtrey were a bit too old for such goings-on. Charles Daughtrey was over 90, and his wife was "older'n' that." Their teen-aged grandson, Cleveland Harmon, however, was just the proper age to attract a poltergeist.

As if the animated bedclothes were the signal to attack in force, Mrs. Daughtrey had found herself dodging a falling bedroom dresser and a flying vase before she could escape from the room that had gone insane. Things were no better out in the kitchen. A bottle of insecticide shot out from under the washing machine and struck Mrs. Daughtrey on the back of her head. The doors to a kitchen cabinet swung open and the salt and pepper shakers popped out.

It was four o'clock in the afternoon and young Cleveland had just returned from school. He was dumped out of his chair in the living room and his homework spiraled in the air as if caught up by a small whirlwind.

"What is going on in here?" asked a neighbor, who had pushed open the screendoor. She had been convinced by the shouting and screaming that she had heard coming from the Daughtreys that the family was being attacked by a gang of hoodlums. When the neighbor entered the house, she was startled to see a pipe and a tin of tobacco float out of a bedroom and drift on down the hallway to the kitchen.

The police arrived early that evening, fully equipped with the standard theories of pranksters and prowlers. To aid in their investigation, the lawmen brought along a police dog. The dog wasn't able to sniff out any practical joker, but the officer handling the canine detective was struck in the leg by an "unidentified flying object."

"You stay around here," the elderly Mrs. Daughtrey nodded sagely, "and you're likely to get hit by a lot of things."

For the next two evenings, always beginning about four o'clock in the afternoon, life in the Daughtrey household became chaos. Books, vases, pens, figurines, kitchen utensils, and several other objects began to orbit about in the poltergeist's Portsmouth domain. Certain pieces of furniture became animated, and the glass in all the windows on one side of the house began to shatter, pane by pane. On Sunday, Cleveland and his grandfather were struck on the chest by tomatoes. Police officers who had been interviewing the two men at the time, testified that they had not seen anyone throw the vegetables, nor had the tomatoes been visible before they struck Charles Daughtrey and his grandson.

A staff writer for the *Norfolk Virginian-Pilot* visited the Daughtreys and spent the afternoon dodging flying cups, tobacco tins, and vases. "I didn't believe in ghosts —until today," the reporter wrote.

As usual, the disturbances attracted the curiosity seekers, the cultists, and the disorderly. The police threw rope cordons around the house to protect the Daughtreys from unsolicited "spook-layers" and posted twelve patrolmen and two dogs on around-the-clock duty until the manifestations subsided.

The Daughtrey's uninvited lodger turned out to have had enough of the policemen and the milling crowds during that hectic weekend. By Monday morning, a patrolman on duty outside of the house reported all quiet. A four-day campaign of chaos had been enough for the Portsmouth poltergeist to have run its course.

THE HAUNTED CHRISTMAS QUILT

IT LOOKS INNOCENT enough. A colorful red and yellow stitched patchwork quilt of the type seen in so many Midwestern farmhomes. This particular quilt happens to be found in the home of Mr. and Mrs. William Monroe of Poy Sippi, Wisconsin, and they claim that it is haunted.

The Monroes found the quilt in 1955 when they moved into the farmhouse which they now occupy. The former tenant had died, and the Monroes had bought the place completely furnished. Mrs. Monroe discovered the quilt folded away in a box and was immediately taken with it, because "it was so beautiful and so old."

She did not remove it from the box for over two years, however, until she decided to put the quilt on her guest bed. It was shortly after this that the Monroes' daughter, Mrs. Florence Delfosse of nearby Oshkosh, arrived for an over-night visit and spent the night in the guest room under the quilt. Or, at least, she was under the quilt for a while.

"A little after midnight, I was awakened by a jerking from the foot end of the old quilt," said Mrs. Delfosse. "I was too frightened to yell, but I held onto the quilt with both hands. The quilt kept pulling, and I heard a voice say: 'Give me back my Christmas quilt!' "

The stubborn Mrs. Delfosse had held onto the quilt until dawn and the cessation of the tugging. "The voice was that of a woman, speaking in a pleasant voice," Mrs. Delfosse remembered. "But she was as determined as I was."

Mrs. Monroe decided that they had acquired a haunted Christmas quilt along with the farmhouse. It was hard to believe by day, as they stood examining the old quilt, but she remembered that she had had some strange feelings about the quilt almost from the first moment that she had discovered it. The Monroes resolved to say nothing about the strange behavior of the quilt and to simply treat it as their "family ghost." It wasn't long, though, before another daughter, Mrs. Margaret Lowther, came to test the quilt.

Mrs. Lowther, accompanied by her own daughter, flung the quilt off the bed shortly after midnight when it became "as hot as an oven."

Eighteen-year-old Tom Lowther was the next to accept the challenge of sleeping under the peculiar quilt. While his cousin, Richard Hobbs, also eighteen, watched from a roll-away bed across the room, Tom snuggled down with the quilt on a davenport.

"Right after midnight, Richard saw the quilt pull itself off the sleeping Tom," Mrs. Monroe later told reporters. "He said the quilt raised about a foot above the sleeping boy and just floated toward the foot end of the davenport and landed on the floor."

By now, the fame of the "crazy Christmas quilt" had spread. A boyfriend of the Monroe's granddaughter offered to take the quilt home for a personal trial. He later reported that he had set himself the task of watching the quilt all night long. About midnight, he said, the quilt had started to move. When he jumped out of bed so that he might better watch the activity of the old quilt, the cover straightened itself out upon his bed until it was as smooth as if no one had yet disturbed it. The young man's tale became a bit dramatic when he went on to add that a "faceless man wearing a farmer's hat" had knocked at his door.

Others who took a turn sleeping under the Christmas quilt claimed that they could hear "the sounds of a heart beating."

At last, William Monroe announced that he would brave the night with the quilt on his own bed. "The quilt began to tug," Monroe said, "and at first I decided to hang on. Then I thought, why not let go and see what the blamed thing was up to. The crazy thing dragged itself across the floor and curled up under the dresser."

"I believe him," Mrs. Monroe said later. "He called me and the quilt was cross the floor and under the dresser. My husband was the bravest of all, but he doesn't want that quilt on his bed any more."

A cousin living in Oakland, California wrote and asked to try out the quilt. She returned the quilt after a few weeks with a letter stating that the quilt had become very hot whenever anyone tried to sleep under it. She also reported the sounds of footsteps, like "someone running around the house in his barefeet" while they had the quilt in their home.

On Halloween night, 1963, five ladies gathered to put the haunted quilt of Poy Sippi to the ultimate test. Nancy McCue, a correspondent for the *Oshkosh Northwestern,* was the spokesman for the feminine ring of "ghost-breakers." Two of the ladies were assigned the task of sleeping in a bed covered with the Christmas quilt while the other three women were to stand guard and keep a sharp eye ready for anything suspicious or supernormal. Evidently the formidable gathering of the five women was too much for the ghost or poltergeist that had become possessive toward the quilt. "In spite of all compliance with actions previously associated with the quilt, nothing happened which any of us observed or felt," Mrs. McCue officially reported.

The professional debunkers and certain psychologists began to make newsprint with their tidy analyses that attributed the quilt's antics to "group hysteria." The fact that the Monroe family had experienced the phenomenon of the curious quilt for more than six years before they began to talk about it in public seems to make that explanation just a bit too pat and superficial. There are those who have slept under the quilt who swear that the tugging and the protesting voice seemed all too real to be dismissed by sophistication.

THERE'S SOMEONE IN THE CELLAR

MR. AND MRS. LINCOLN live with their two sons, John, 22, and Tom, 15, in an old frame house in Jackson, Michigan. The Lincolns enjoy the quiet life—peaceful evenings at home with the family grouped together in the living room. It was just such an evening in September, 1961, when Mrs. Lincoln raised her head from the book that she was reading and said softly to her son, John: "Listen. There's someone in the cellar."

John turned his attention from the television set that had been adjusted to a low volume and tilted his head to test his mother's statement. Tiny pin pricks of fear and excitement jabbed his spine. His mother was right.

There were distinct sounds of someone moving around in the cellar.

John alerted his father, who had gone upstairs for a moment, and Mr. Lincoln answered the alarm by hurrying down the stairs with a loaded shotgun. He pushed open the cellar door, clicked on the lights, demanded that whoever was down there show himself at once.

There was only silence from the cellar, and, as the menfolk descended the staircase, they could see that the basement was completely empty. But everyone commented how strange it was that their dog which had taken one sniff at the cellar steps, ran to hide itself under the divan.

By the next evening, weird, wind-like noises began to howl up from the cellar. Dishes at the dinner table began to slide off the table; cutlery began to bounce into the air. Doors opened and closed when no human hand was near.

The Lincolns are a non-musical family, so they, of course, had no musical instruments in the house. Yet on several occasions, they heard an organ pealing "Rock of Ages" and other hymns. In addition to the invisible organ and its equally invisible organist, the Lincolns were also treated to a number of selections by a ghostly trumpeter, an other-wordly accordianist, and even a bit of bonny Scotland by an ethereal bagpiper.

For several months the Lincolns endured the antics of their unseen lodger. The manuevers of the poltergeist were all of an annoying rather than harmful nature, and once the thing had even helped Mrs. Lincoln with the housework by making the beds. However, as Mrs. Lincoln was all alone in the house at the time, she had become more terrified than grateful toward her invisible housemaid.

On February 1, 1962, the older son, John, had occasion to regret his attempts at castigating the poltergeist. As John prepared for bed, the steel wall locker containing his clothes fell slowly to the floor. Irritated by this tactic, John began abusing the ghostly prankster with every strong name that came to his tongue. Evidently the thing did not appreciate the young man's verbal abuse, and it hurled a bottle of hair dressing at his head. John managed to duck, and, with astonished eyes, he watched

109

the bottle veer sharply to the right, continue to fly out into the dining room, smash a window, then fall to the floor.

The sickness in the Lincoln house lasted for well over a year, and neighbors and various officials witnessed the flying bottles, noisy winds, and falling cupboards that had made the fifty-year-old family home become a house of psychic unrest.

THE COP WHO CHASED A GHOST

APPARENTLY a poltergeist can sometimes be "cured" by a good shock treatment if it is administered by the proper agent. In October, 1964, in Montreal, Canada, the city's favorite cop, Detective-Sergeant Leo Plouffe, performed a psychic *coup de gras* to an apartment that had been plagued by a persistent poltergeist.

The apartment was rented by Mr. and Mrs. Wilfred Payfer and their three young sons. Payfer, who works in a shoe factory, is a quiet religious man. The last thing in the world that Wilfred Payfer would want would be to create any kind of a disturbance or to gain any kind of notoriety. He was almost apologetic when he told his landlord about the loud knocks that had sounded night after night over the bed of his children.

The pounding, Payfer told his landlord, had begun on August 9th, at nine o'clock. Since that night, the disturbance always started at the same time, just shortly after eight-year-old Robert, seven-year-old Guy, and four-year-old Richard had fallen asleep. On occasion, the wall had trembled violently. Once a crucifix was knocked off a wall; another time the bangings had caused a breeze strong enough to rumple Mrs. Payfer's hair.

Neighbors had heard it and had complained to the Payfers right from the start. A woman living next door had moved out when the Payfers convinced her that they were powerless to stop the nocturnal knockings.

The landlord came and heard for himself. He became so intrigued that he tore down the mysterious wall, had the plumbing and wiring checked, found nothing, ordered the wall rebuilt.

"It's beyond me," the landlord admitted when the

knockings resumed. "If you want to move, I'll cancel your lease."

The Payfers moved, and for two nights enjoyed an escape from the terrible bangings. Mrs. Payfer, who had been under a physician's care since the disturbances began, allowed herself to relax. Then, on September 7th, the knockings had located them at their new apartment on rue Ernest-Gendreau. This time things were worse. The story of their pesky poltergeist had got around, and crowds began to gather every night in the narrow street outside their apartment. A priest arrived and tried to exorcise what Payfer insisted upon calling their "evil spirits." The clergyman failed to silence the rappings and suggested that the Payfers call the police.

Two tough, veteran cops were assigned to the case, but the ghostly noises made the officers blanch as white as any rookies. One policeman got so nervous that he unholstered his revolver, and the other—a burly officer who had been engaged in several gun fights with desperate criminals—became so frightened that he ran out of the apartment and into the street.

Newspaper and television reporters began to have a field day with the Payfer's private ghost. Radio reporters aimed microphones at the bedroom wall and were gratified to hear a series of bangs sound right on cue. One radio station gave minute-to-minute bulletins on the affair, broadcasting tape-recorded knockings for the titillation of its listeners. The French-language tabloids spread the story across their front pages.

The police conducted an experiment by leading the Payfers back to their old apartment. The children had no sooner stepped into the flat when the walls began banging out a welcome.

The crowds outside the Payfers' apartment had become so huge that the police blocked off traffic and alerted civil defense units. Wildred Payfer complained that the family had received plenty of crude publicity but no relief from the nightly chorus of knockings.

It was at this point that Detective-Sergeant Leo Plouffe entered the drama. Plouffe, who gained national attention in Canada with his investigation of scores of separtist bombing scares and his subsequent dismantling of several lethal bombs, took time out from working on

111

his M.A. in criminology to handle the case. The no-nonsense Detective-Sergeant arrived at nine o'clock, the regular witching hour for the manifestations, and took charge at once. He shoo-ed everyone but the Payfer family out of the apartment and made himself comfortable for an all-night vigil beside the mysterious wall. Next to his easy chair was a sensitive microphone and a radio transmitter.

"If you want to observe a psychic phenomenon," he explained to a reporter, "you've got to do it right."

The Payfer children slumbered on undisturbed as the wall above their beds remained silent. Detective-Sergeant Plouffe stifled a yawn. Evidently he had broken the chain of psychic energy; if, indeed, he grumbled, there had ever been one.

About midnight, Plouffe got up to turn on a light in the darkened flat. "From outside," the officer later said, "there came a roar like you hear at the Forum when Bellveau scores a goal. There must have been five thousand people out there, and when they saw the light in the window they thought they'd seen a ghost."

Shortly after dawn, Plouffe gathered his "ghost-hunting" equipment and stalked out of the apartment building in disgust. "The only rappings I heard all night came from a radio reporter banging on the window to find out what was going on.

"I really got the idea," Plouffe shook his head in bewilderment, "that I was the only sane person in the place. The whole affair is an object-lesson in mass hysteria."

Although the tough-minded Detective-Sergeant had passed the night unmolested and the apartment has entertained no wall-bangings since his vigil, one cannot completely discount the testimony of the Payfers, the priests, the other policemen, and the journalists who swear that they really did hear something knocking on the wall. It may just be that the fearless cop was psychically powerful enough to conduct his own one-man poltergeist purge.

THE POLTERGEIST OF SLAWENSIK

COUNCILLOR August Hahn sadly shook the hand of his employer and patron, Prince Friedrich Ludwig von Hohenlohe, and hoped that it would be *auf weidersehen* and not goodbye. The Prussian armies had been mauled by the military genius of Napoleon and the zeal of his French army. The battle of Jena had been lost, and just three weeks after the declaration of war between Prussia and France, Prince Hohenlohe had surrendered his army at Prezlau on October 28, 1806.

Prince Friedrich Hohenlohe had been declared a prisoner of war and was being taken to France until Napoleon decided either to ransom him or to set him free. "You have been paroled," Prince Friedrich had told August Hahn over their farewell handshake, "but I ask you to grant me one last order."

"You have but to ask," Councillor Hahn said. "Tell me how I may serve you."

Prince Friedrich smiled, pleased with his employee's loyalty. "I should like very much for us to return home together. Would you remain at my castle, Slawensik, in Upper Silesia until I can join you there? The French can't keep me prisoner forever."

Although he was eager to return to his home, August Hahn's admiration for the Prince demanded that he accept the charge. He had never visited this particular castle before, but as the Prince had numerous estates, this was not unusual. Hahn would be certain of the company of Johannes, his personal servant, two of the Prince's coachmen, and Frau Knittel, the caretaker, who lived on the grounds with her son. In addition to the servants, however, Councillor Hahn wanted to insure his having some intellectual fellowship. He entreated his boyhood friend, Karl Kern, who had been at Jena as a member of a Hussar regiment, to join him at the castle until they might return home with their Prince. Kern consented to become a member of the group of self-imposed exiles, and the entourage arrived at Castle Slawensik on November 19, 1806.

"It's not the most attractive building in the world,

is it?" Councillor Hahn asked his friend as he surveyed the crumbling medieval castle.

"I don't suppose the Prince wanted you to be too comfortable while he was being held a prisoner of war," Kern laughed.

The two young men occupied a corner room on the first floor. "At any rate," Hahn sighed, "I've brought several books and an excellent collection of Schiller's poetry."

"Schiller is the perfect antidote for boredom," Kern said, voicing his approval of his friend's thoughtfulness in bringing books. Especially a volume of Schiller, who was their favorite poet. To thwart boredom, the two friends decided to spend the evenings reading selections of Schiller's poetry aloud.

It was about nine o'clock on the third evening following their arrival at Slawensik that they were interrupted in their reading by a shower of lime that fell over the room.

"The place is coming down around our ears," Karl Kern said, jumping to his feet. "The old medieval monstrosity is about to collapse!"

Councillor Hahn glanced warily toward the ceiling. "But that's peculiar. Where's the crack that all this lime came from?"

The two friends stood up on chairs so that they might better inspect the ceiling. They were unable to detect one single sign of damage.

Hahn frowned at the ceiling, then at the bits of lime that had showered down on them. "The lime unquestionably came from the ceiling. But how?"

His question was met with another fall of pieces of lime.

"Did you see where they came from that time?" he asked Kern, who was stooping to pick up fresh specimens.

"No," Kern said. "But they feel very cold to the touch, as if they've somehow loosened themselves from an outside wall."

Councillor Hahn continued to study the ceiling for some kind of opening through which the lime might have dropped. "We'll have to see to it first thing in the morning," he said. "We may have to put the servants to work with some repairing before the winter weather gets any worse."

The next morning, the young men's room was nearly completely carpeted by the mysterious lime.

"Good lord," Kern said, shaking out his bedclothes. "This is terrible. The ceiling could have fallen in on us last night!"

"But where are the cracks?" Councillor Hahn asked, dropping his arms sharply to his sides. "There should be huge, gaping cracks to cause so much lime to fall."

That night, the bits of lime did more than fall from an invisible crack. They began to fly about the room and pelt the young men. As they retreated to their beds, the sound of loud knockings began to reverberate eerily down the ancient halls of the castle.

"Stop it!" Kern shouted, sitting up in his bed. "August Hahn stop whatever you are doing! For some reason, you are trying to frighten me. While I am looking away, you pelt me with bits of lime. And now, somehow, you are making that terrible banging. Perhaps you are banging on your bedstead, eh?"

Kern got out of bed and approached his friend. "I demand to inspect your bed! Somewhere I'll find your little pile of lime, and I'll discover how you are making that noise!"

Then, while both of Hahn's hands were in full view of his nervous and angry companion, a loud series of knocks shook the room. Kern lowered his eyes sheepishly. "I'm sorry, August," he apologized. "I knew that you were not responsible, yet I simply had to satisfy myself. Since the war, I have been somewhat nervous."

Hahn got out of bed, put an arm around the shoulder of his friend. "There is no need to apologize. I was about to cross over to your bed and accuse you of the same thing."

The loud raps on the wall made sleep virtually impossible. August Hahn brought out his notebook and made use of his sleeplessness by beginning a journal of the phenomena. A graduate attorney, Hahn was not a man who could be easily deceived or taken in by the work of a prankster. As an added measure to help insure his objectivity in the recording of the Slawensik disturbances, Hahn wrote his journal in the third person.

115

When the manifestations began on the next night, Hahn and Kern were ready with the keys to the rooms overhead. While Hahn remained below, Kern and the son of the caretaker went to search the apartments above their rooms. All the rooms were empty.

"It appears that Prince Friedrich owns a haunted castle," Hahn laughed when Kern and Knittel returned with their report.

His joke seemed hollow, indeed, when they were awakened later that night by the sounds of slippered feet moving across the room. A lighted candle showed the room to be empty. Before the evening had ended, the invisible slippers had been joined by what sounded like a walking stick, bouncing on one end. Councillor Hahn maintained a running commentary of facetious remarks, but Kern knew that his friend's apparent levity was a device to keep both of them from fleeing the castle in terror.

Within another night, the young men and the servants had stopped trying to explain the disturbances in terms of natural causes. Candlesticks had begun to fly from one corner of the room to another. When they sat down to dinner, knives, forks, plates, and foodstuffs became animated and airborne. Anything movable seemed to be possessed with the greatest desire to fly about the room.

"Well," Kern sighed, as a piece of soap with which he was about to wash his hands jumped out of his reach. "At least that infernal pounding has stopped."

The determined young men attempted sleep in their room for three weeks before they gave the servants orders to have their things moved into the corner room overhead. "If there's such a thing as a haunted room," Hahn said, "then this must surely be an excellent example. We've tried for three weeks to outlast whatever force persists in this room. Now we've got to get a good night's sleep."

That night, Hahn and Kern wearily disrobed for bed. "This has to work," Councillor Hahn yawned. "The ghost can have the room downstairs to itself."

"This is odd," Kern said. "I'm certain I left this book downstairs in the library."

116

"You probably brought it up with your fresh nightshirt and simply forgot about it."

"But here is your pipe. Didn't you give it to Johannes to clean?"

"Of course I did," Hahn frowned. "He can't have returned it already."

Alerted to peculiarity, the young men looked about the room and noticed several articles from other parts of the castle that had suddenly appeared among their effects. Then a series of loud raps sounded on the wall above Kern's bed. Their favorite collection of Schiller leaped up from a night table. A lighted candle sailed across the room from one dresser to another.

"Oh, no!" Hahn said, drawing the bedclothes up over his head. "Let them fling as they will. I must have some sleep at all costs!"

The Councillor had not slept long when he was awakened by the sound of his friend whimpering. Hahn rolled out of bed and saw Kern staring into a mirror as though he were transfixed. He was extremely pale and trembling as if suffering from a high fever. Hahn draped a coat about his shoulders and led him to his bed.

"In the mirror," Kern managed at last, "clearly reflected, I saw a feminine figure all swathed in white. At first I thought it was my imagination, but I could see my own reflection behind the ghostly woman. The phantasm's eyes met my own. The face was that of an old woman. Her features appeared quite tranquil and not at all disagreeable, but I could not help being filled with some sort of nameless dread."

Hahn stepped to the mirror and demanded that the shade show itself to him. He stared into the mirror for fifteen minutes before he finally abandoned his attempts to summon the apparition.

By now it was nearly dawn, and the young men forgot about sleep for another night. As soon as they heard the servants stirring, Hahn said, "There's no advantage to sleeping up here. We might just as well have our things brought back down."

While Hahn and Kern sat to their breakfasts, the coachmen were sent to transport their effects back down to the original corner apartment. Within a few moments, the servants had come back to the table. "We can't get the door open, sir," one of them announced.

"It's not locked," Kern said. "Of course you can get the door open."

The servants nodded obediently and went off to try the door again. They were back a second time and a third time before Councillor Hahn grew weary of the routine and accompanied them up to the apartment. At his slightest touch, the door swung freely open. He turned to face the servants, his arms folded across his chest, his forehead wrinkled in a frown.

"I swear upon my honor that both of us pushing together couldn't budge that door an inch," one of the coachmen said. The other quickly added his own oath, so Hahn could do nothing but believe that some preternatural force had prevented the two burly men from entering the apartment.

Another month passed at Slawensik castle, and weird tales of unearthly happenings began to be spread abroad. Two Bavarian officers, Captain Cornet and Lieutenant Nagerle, both hard-nosed skeptics, decided to come out to the castle and see what all the ghost business was about. Lieutenant Nagerle, the most vocal in his skepticism, offered to spend a night in the haunted corner room.

"Are you certain that you know what you're letting yourself in for?" Karl Kern asked the brash officer.

"I'm ready for whatever pranks your noisy ghost wants to try on me," the lieutenant laughed.

The men had not left the Bavarian officer for more than a few minutes when they heard the lieutenant cursing loudly. The usual noises of the disturbance were punctuated by the sounds of the officer's saber hacking away at table and chairs.

"We'd better go rescue Lieutenant Nagerle!" Captain Cornet exclaimed.

"And our furniture," Kern said.

When they opened the door to the room that the poltergeist had claimed for its own, they were shocked to see Lieutenant Nagerle chopping at the air with his saber. It was difficult to believe that the officer, who moments before had been so cynical and brave, was now reduced to a frightened man who ran about an empty room, slashing at an invisible enemy.

At the sight of his companions entering the bedroom, Lieutenant Nagerle seemed to shake off his fear and replace it with anger. "As soon as you left me, the accursed thing started to pelt me. I looked everywhere, but could see nothing. I'm afraid my anger got the best of me, and I drew my saber."

Once again in control of his faculties, the lieutenant began to suggest that he might somehow have been tricked by Councillor Hahn and Karl Kern. The two friends sat down with the officers and earnestly sought to convince them that they were guilty of no connivance. Captain Cornet also assured his fellow officer that he had not allowed Hahn and Kern out of his sight. Then, while the men sat talking around the table, the candle snuffers rose in mid-air and fell to the floor. A lead ball struck Hahn on the chest, but without harming him. The sound of footsteps began to pad about the room, and a drinking glass jumped off a stand to shatter itself against the floor.

Lieutenant Nagerle shrugged his shoulders, sat for a few moments in stunned silence, then admitted: "This is all completely impossible, but I can't believe this is caused by either of you."

The phenomena at Slawensik castle continued to increase in strength and ingenuity. Once, after August Hahn had carefully prepared some water for shaving and had heated it to just the temperature that he desired, the warm water was sucked out of the basin before he was able to moisten his razor.

Herr Doerfel, a local bookseller, had his hat hidden from him as he was preparing to leave the castle. After the household had looked for several minutes in vain, Herr Doerfel's hat was seen to float teasingly in front of its owner. As the frustrated and frightened bookseller reached for his head piece, the hat jerked out of his grasp. With Herr Doerfel running in pursuit, the hat led its owner a merry chase before it finally dropped at his feet.

Councillor Hahn, who was nearly prostrate from lack of sleep, announced firmly to the entity one night that he did not want to feel a single object thrown at him while he attempted to rest on his bed. It seemed for a little while as though the thing was going to co-operate with Hahn. The Councillor had just drifted off into a deep sleep when he was rudely awakened by a large quantity of water being dumped in his face. At least the poltergeist hadn't thrown any objects.

One of the most eerie of the phenomena occured during the absence of Councillor Hahn, who had left the castle for a few days to journey to Breslau. Kern, who was nervous throughout the disturbances, refused to sleep alone in the haunted room, but was just stubborn enough to refuse to move his bed to another. At last, he persuaded Johannes, Hahn's personal servant, to spend the night with him in the afflicted bedroom.

They had not been settled long before they saw a jug of beer rise slowly from a table and begin to pour its beverage into a tumbler. Then, before their unbelieving eyes, the glass was lifted and began to empty, just as if someone were there drinking. "Good lord!" the terrified Johannes whispered in a hoarse voice, "it swallows!"

The glass was replaced on the table, and the men walked quickly to the place where the "thing" had drunk. There was not a drop of beer to be found on the floor.

The disturbances seemed to culminate with the beer-drinking episode. One night, as Hahn was returning home to the castle, he began to hear the footpads of a dog behind him. Thinking it was their greyhound, Flora, the Councillor turned and called the dog by name. There was nothing to be seen. He continued walking, still hearing the sound of a dog following close at foot. Even when he ascended the stairs, he could still hear the dog panting at his heels.

Kern met him at the door, taking the door-knob from his friend's hand and calling the name of their greyhound.

"Do you see a dog?" Hahn asked his friend.

"Why, of course, I see a dog," Kern replied, looking more and more puzzled as he continued to search the step and the stairs for Flora. "Certainly I did. Flora was close behind you—half within the door—and that was the reason I took hold of the knob. You seemed not to see her, and I was afraid that you might shut the door on her."

Hahn explained to Kern about the mysterious footfalls of the invisible dog that had been following him in the dark.

Kern shook his head in awe. "I had been watching you come up the path. I saw a dog walking behind you. It was a white dog, and I took it for Flora."

The two friends immediately began a search for the greyhound. If one of them had *heard* a dog, and the other had *seen* one, surely Flora must now be scampering about in the woods. They found Flora locked up in the stables. The coachmen assured them that the dog had not been set free at anytime during the day.

After this strange incident, the manifestations at Slawensik came to a halt. Councillor Hahn remained at the old castle for another six months until his employer, Prince Hohenlohe was released from his imprisonment in France. Hahn concluded his journal with the words: "I have described these events exactly as I heard and saw them; from beginning to end I observed them with the most entire self-possession . . . yet the whole thing remains to me perfectly inexplicable. Written the 19th November, 1808."

Hahn did not seek to publish his bizarre journal until twenty years had passed. At that time, he submitted the manuscript to Dr. Andreas Justinus Kerner, the lyric poet, physician, chemist, and pioneer parapsychologist. When Kerner published the journal, it created an immediate sensation in Germany.

The only key to the mystery—and it was a nebulous "supernatural" one at best—came in 1830 when Slawensik was destroyed by a fire that had been caused by the direct hit of a lightning bolt. In the ruins, workmen discovered the skeleton of a man who had been walled up in a secret enclosure. His skull had been split and a sword lay by his side.

When Councillor Hahn was told of the strange discovery, he wrote: "One may imagine some connection between the skeleton, the female image seen by Kern, and the disturbances we witnessed. But who can really know? It does not matter to me whether others believe my story or not. I clearly recollect what I myself thought of such matters before I had actually witnessed them. Nor do I think ill of anyone who passes the same judgment of me that I would have passed previous to my own experiences."

We have already seen in earlier chapters how persons of the right telepathic affinity may have the ability to stir up the psychic residue of emotions that have lain dormant for years. Before we are content to accept the Slawensik phenomena as completely without explanation, let us remember that Frau Knittel, the caretaker, lived on the grounds with a son just entering puberty. It may also be pertinent to note that Karl Kern died of a nervous disorder about a year after the disturbances had ceased. It was Kern who was the most upset and nervous about the phenomena, and it should be remembered that Kern was the only one who "saw" the figure of the lady and the white dog. It may well have been that Kern had suffered some severe psychic shock in the war, and the tremors remained powerful enough to revive terrible emotions that had lingered within the dank and crumbling castle.

THE ARMY STORE'S WALKING BOOTS

WHEN MR. SHARP took over the army surplus store on that Monday morning, he was still bewildered by the former proprieter's odd behavior and the weird story that he had told as he handed over the keys on the previous Friday.

The man had actually seemed reluctant to allow Mr. Sharp to take ownership of the Lancashire, England shop—not because of any regrets about selling the store, but because he seemed to fear for Mr. Sharp's well-being. His story had been strange. He told Mr. Sharp that, as he readied the store for new ownership, he had heard peculiar noises coming from the upper floor. It had seemed as though someone were walking around up there, and the longer he walked, the bigger and heavier he became. By late afternoon, the footsteps sounded as if they were those of a giant. The man was certain that there was no one upstairs and that there had been no one up there all day. When it came time to catch the evening train, he had realized that his coat was on the upper floor. He had started for the stairway, then as a particularly violent bump sounded, he bolted and left the store on the run.

Mr. Sharp was puzzled by the man's story. He had known the fellow for several years, knew that he was an ex-commando who had taken part in some of the bloodiest campaigns of World War II. It was indeed difficult to imagine the man running from some silly bumps on the floor. Obviously the poor fellow was breaking up. It was a good thing that he had decided to retire.

Mr. Sharp was soon to learn, however, that whatever his friend had heard clomping around in the upper room, it could hardly be written off so lightly as "a case of nerves."

He later told newsmen: "It was shortly after I had taken over the store, and I was working late one evening. I heard distinctly the steady tread of footsteps on the floor above. I knew that there was no one but myself in the shop. I ran out of the store to see if there was anybody about next door. The place was deserted.

"I was determined to find out what was going on, and I started to run up the stairs. As I reached the third step, my legs seemed suddenly to freeze. I looked up and sensed, more than saw, a figure walking along the small passageway at the top of the stairs. I admit that I was really frightened!"

The next morning when Mr. Sharp opened up the surplus store, he was dismayed to find that several shelves of army ankle-boots, which had been carefully stacked the previous afternoon, had been scattered about the shop. His first thought was that a burglar had broken into the shop and, finding only a few coins in the cash register, had decided to express his disappointment by an act of vandalism. He checked the back door and all windows, but could discover no way by which an interloper might have gained entrance to the store.

It wasn't until he discovered the boots dumped about the floor on the next morning that Mr. Sharp began to connect the mysterious "walking" on the upper floor with the senseless violation of his shelves. The pattern was repeated on several mornings, until Mr. Sharp could

123

plan on his picking up the scattered boots as a matter of course.

One night, when he stayed after the closing hour to catch up on some book work, he was startled to feel the pressure of a hand on his shoulder. He spun around on his chair, but there was no one there—only the sound of retreating footsteps.

Eventually, rumors of strange goings-on in the army surplus store began to reach the ears of inquisitive newsmen. With the permission of Mr. Sharp, some reporters from the Lancashire *Evening Post* decided to maintain an evening's vigil in the shop. One newsman assured him that there was a perfectly normal explanation for the seemingly odd occurrences and that they would have the cause of his "walking boots" ready for simple explanation on the following morning.

One of the newsman wrote that the journalists carefully inspected the upper rooms and found them to be completely empty. Because of his reluctance to enter the area after dark, Mr. Sharp had long since ceased using the area for storage. The reporters were also careful to test the rooms for loose boards, noisy shutters, or gnawing rats.

"Throughout the evening, we heard a great variety of sounds," wrote a reporter, "especially heavy bumping and thumping sounds. At other times there were noises like metal scraping the floor.

"It was just after midnight when we seemed to hear the sound of a chain being rattled across the floor. By this time, we were all quite nervous. We were convinced that we were not hearing rats and mice, nor the antics of some jokester."

Shortly after midnight, most of the journalists left the noisy upper floor for the comparative quiet of the shop area. With the coming of dawn and the cessation of the activity, the reporters made another inspection of the storage rooms. They were amazed to discover a long chain lying in one corner of a room. They all agreed that there had been no chain in any of the storage rooms when they made their first inspection. Upon opening a closet door, a reporter called the attention of his fellow journalists to a broken, three-legged chair that they had previously noted as hanging from one of a series of wall pegs. It now dangled from one of the other pegs on the closet wall.

Each of the newsmen accused the other of having crept up and moved it. While they were arguing over which one had played ghost, Mr. Sharp arrived and put the clincher on their debate. He swore that when he had left that previous evening, there had been no chair at all in the upper floor. Nor, he insisted, had he ever seen that particular chair before in his life.

When the journalists left the army surplus store that morning, they had to confess that rather than solving any mystery, they had merely complicated it.

Although the thing that inhabited the upper floor had contented itself with entertaining the journalists during their overnight stay, by the next morning it had reverted to raising havoc with Mr. Sharp's merchandise. The harried shopkeeper opened his door that next day to find boxes emptied of their contents, army boots strewn about the shop, shirts unpinned and draped across shelves, and trouser legs tied together in knots.

Frank Spencer, a British clairvoyant, paid a visit to the haunted army store and later told reporters that he had "seen" a number of entities inhabiting the building. Each of these entities had wailed of an injustice or a great sorrow that kept it earthbound. Investigation later revealed that the surplus store had been built on the site of an ancient jail. An unused section of the basement was found to be paved with flagstones and contained an old room that may very well have been an old cell.

When last interviewed in the spring of 1952, Mr. Sharp was less concerned about "who" or "what" was causing the disturbance in his store than he was with "why they insist upon making such a terrible mess of my shop."

THE POLTERGEIST THAT CAME TO THE OFFICE

WHEN JIM HAZELWOOD, editorial writer for the Oakland *Tribune*, arrived at the office of court reporter George Wheeler at 1904 Franklin Street on June 15, 1964 the poltergeist had already been active for two weeks.

The first manifestations, according to Mrs. Helen

Rosenberg, concerned themselves with the telephones in the office. The row of lights on each telephone base would light up in rapid succession, but there would be no one on the line. The telephone company insisted that there was nothing wrong with the instruments.

The disturbances centered next on the electric typewriters. The coil springs beneath the keys began to go limp, twisted together, and balled up. When the repairmen came to take them away, they left replacement machines in order that work in the office might go on without interruption. The springs on the loan machines, however, began to suffer from the same mysterious mechanical affliction. When the original typewriters were returned to Wheeler's office, their springs once again began to twist and bend.

Bob Goosey, a sales representative for the Royal McBee typewriter company told Hazelwood: "Those springs normally last for the life of the machine. We haven't replaced three of those springs in the last 10 years. But during the past few days, we've replaced about 100 in Wheeler's machines. We've practically exhausted our stock of springs in the Bay area."

Hazelwood arrived at the office about fifteen minutes after Officer Charles Nye had completed an inspection tour of the suite. The inhabitants of the beseiged office had decided to suffer in silence no longer. The staff members of Wheeler's office included, in addition to himself, his wife Zolo, court reporters Robert Caya and Calvert Bowles, and two transcribers, Helen Rosenberg and John Orfanides.

Zolo Wheeler took the reporter to her husband's office while Wheeler was out for the moment. The room was in a shambles. A cracked ashtray littered the floor along with a pile of smashed crockery. A puddle of water had seeped out of a broken flower vase that rested against a corner of Wheeler's desk.

"When I arrived," Officer Nye told Hazelwood, "that vase was on a shelf 18-inches deep. It flew across the room and made a right turn to get where it is now."

While the policeman spoke, he was interrupted by a banging sound from the room on the left. One of the telephones had fallen to the floor. "We got tired of picking up telephones," Hazelwood later wrote. "While I was in Wheeler's office on June 15th, all eight of the phones kept sliding off the desks and falling to the floor with monotonous regularity."

Jim Edelen, a staff photographer for the *Tribune*, arrived and asked John Orfanides to pose beside a pile of debris. Edelen snapped the picture, and the two men turned to leave the room. Their attention was brought sharply back to the debris when they heard a loud crash behind them. The floor was now covered with white powder. A large jar of powdered cream substitute had jumped out of the coffee cupboard and smashed on the floor.

The phenomena called a halt to its unwelcome activities at precisely four o'clock. George Wheeler announced that he was going to move some of his equipment into an empty office downstairs in an attempt to escape the wild "thing." It was imperative that the staff get caught up on work that had been accumulating because of the poltergeist's rampages.

The next day, Wheeler's frustrations were multiplied when he learned that the "office pest" had followed them into the new suite. In addition, Wheeler had brought grief to other offices on the second floor. Ralph and Jeanetta Ryan, who run an engineering insurance service, had their typewriter bound off a desk and several coffee cups explode. Their telephone hurled to the floor and was broken.

In another office on the second floor, dental technician Frank Bacigalupi was mixing some paste when an asbestos board suddenly tore loose from the nails holding it to the wall and fell at his elbow.

Reporter Hazelwood arrived shortly after ten o'clock and went up to the third floor office where some of the staff were still trying valiantly to conduct business. The journalist resolved to keep a logbook of the occurrences for one hour. The journal of those sixty incredible minutes on that Tuesday in June reads as follows:

10:30 A.M. Metal dictaphone foot pedal with cord wrapped around it flew out of the cabinet, struck a wooden counter and fell to the floor. Bob Caya, of Mr. Wheeler's office, was in the room, but was talking on the telephone and had his back to the cabinet.

10:35 A.M. Light bulbs broke in stairwell between

third and fourth floors. Base of bulb was on the stairs with the glass, indicating that it had been unscrewed. No footsteps heard or anyone seen in hallways.

10:40 A.M. Heard noise in Mr. Wheeler's office which was vacant. Discovered can of liquid wax on floor, about eight feet from cupboard where it is kept.

10:45 A.M. Loud noise in vacant office where water cooler is kept. Rushed in immediately to find metal cup container lying on floor approximately 10 feet from cooler. Paper cups were strewn around the floor. No chance for anyone to leave the room without being seen by me.

10:50 A.M. Door which had been removed from hinges on the previous day to permit moving desks, suddenly toppled over with a loud crash. Earlier, I had observed it to be propped against a wall corner at about a 30-degree angle.

11:05 A.M. I was standing in the office doorway when a metal card index file, about three feet behind me, landed on the floor with a loud bang. It had been sitting on a metal filing case where I had placed it earlier. There was no one in the room. The first thing that I had done on entering the office that morning had been to place the index metal box on top of the filing case to see if it would fall. It did.

11:10 A.M. Metal and plastic top of a typewriter flew out of the open window of an office directly beneath us and clattered to the street below where Dr. F. J. Stryble was walking. Dr. Stryble returned the typewriter top to us.

11:13 A.M. Arrival of two physicists with equipment for testing radiation. They found none.

11:20 A.M. A two-pound can of coffee flew out of the cupboard and landed about 10 feet from the shelves in Mr. Wheeler's office. The plastic top of the can came loose and about a handful of coffee was spilled. I was the first one in the room. There was no one there.

In the midst of all this turbulent activity, Irv Dickey, a former president of the California Society for Psychical Study, stepped into the office to investigate. Dickey acclaimed the disturbances, "a classic poltergeist case except for one thing. When the poltergeist phenomenon occurs, it is usually in the presence of an adolescent child. If the child is removed from the location, the phenomenon stops. In this case, there doesn't seem to be a child involved."

By now the newspaper stories were beginning to attract the attention of that unfortunate by-product of poltergeistic phenomena, the curiosity seeker. Crowds of people began to come up to the office to catch a glimpse of the noisy spook. An occultist from San Francisco brought incense in little brass jars and stared soulfully at the ceiling in an attempt to "drive away the evil spirits."

Dr. Arthur Hastings, who was also active in investigating the phenomena at Millville, Iowa, offered his opinion that the office was the scene of "a genuine poltergeist phenomenon." Dr. Hastings told Hazelwood that this was the first time that he had ever heard of a poltergeist case taking place in an office. But the phenomenon was real enough to convince even the most hard-nosed skeptic that this particular poltergeist preferred the typewriters and filing cabinets of an office to the domestic surroundings of a home.

A 30-pound typewriter leaped off a table in an empty room and fell to the floor. A large electric coffee percolator slid off a table and several coffee cups exploded. Bob Goosey, the harrassed typewriter man, saw a heavy wooden filing cabinet turn sideways and fall over.

On Wednesday morning, June 17, the phenomena reached a climax shortly after Cal Bowles and John Orfanides opened the office. In rapid succession, the water cooler tipped over, soaking the left office and covering the floor with broken glass, a large wooden cabinet of office supplies came thudding down, and a movable counter flipped over onto its back.

Jim Hazelwood and Dr. Hastings stood amidst the wreckage that had been caused by the sudden explosion of poltergeistic energy. They were both surprised to learn that John Orfanides had been taken down to police headquarters for questioning. As he moved a bit of glass with the tip of his shoe, Dr. Hastings predicted that the phenomena would not return.

"This is usually the pattern with the poltergeist phenomena," he told Hazelwood. "They start slowly, build up to a climax, and then stop altogether. I don't think

129

we'll see any more of these occurrences. Of course," he added, "I could be wrong."

It appeared at first as though Dr. Hastings' prediction had been accurate. The poltergeist was quiet for nine days, then, on June 26th, it once again punched its psychic timeclock at the Wheeler's office.

"I tried to prepare for it as soon as the first tell-tale signs showed up," Mrs. Zolo Wheeler said. "When springs started breaking in all three typewriters, I knew that it had come back."

Mrs. Wheeler started placing breakable objects on the floor. She had no sooner set a cup down and turned her back than the cup leaped eight feet across the room and shattered against a filing cabinet. Almost simultaneously, two glass ashtrays smashed to the floor, and a stapler bounded from a desktop.

"I don't know what it is," Mrs. Wheeler told Hazelwood, "but we're sick and tired of it."

The editorial writer checked with Dr. Hastings to learn his reaction to the poltergeist's rather impressive comeback. "I still believe that the 'eye of the storm' has passed on and that only the weaker manifestations remain," the Stanford professor said. "Often in cases like this one, there are sporadic incidents, but nothing to the extent that occurred before. The major crisis is over."

It appeared that this time Dr. Hastings was correct. After that last dramatic manifestation, things at the office seemed to quiet down for good. But both Hazelwood and Hastings were shocked when John Orfanides confessed to the police that he had caused all the objects to fall by "flipping them behind his back."

Hazelwood had been away on an assignment in San Francisco on June 29th, the day that the police had called the press conference to air Orfanides' confession. Orfanides had asked to speak with Hazelwood first, but the police had convinced him that he should make his confession public, before reporters from the newspapers. At the press conference, the police had outlined Orfanides' confession, and the 20-year-old court transcriber soberly nodded his head and agreed to the charges that the police read. The story of Orfanides' admission of guilt and trickery went out over all the wire services and was broadcast live on television. Another poltergeist case was "exposed" as the work of a prankster.

Immediately upon his return from San Francisco, Hazelwood started for John Orfanides' apartment, taking Leo Cohen, a staff photographer, along as a witness.

"John," Hazelwood began, "I know and you know that you couldn't have thrown those things around. Isn't that true?"

"Of course I didn't do it," Orfanides said, almost in tears, "but it was easier to admit it and get the police off my back."

The two newsmen informed the police of Orfanides' repudiation of his "confession," but the police had solved the case to their satisfaction and great relief.

"As far as we're concerned," Inspector Matt Roehl said, "the case is closed. Orfanides admitted he did it, explained how he did it; no charges will be filed and that's that!"

Dr. Hastings said that Orfanides could conceivably have caused some of the accidents by trickery, but that there were too many aspects of the case that could not be explained by sleight of hand or by any natural causes. The parapsychologist remains convinced that the Oakland case is a "genuine poltergeist phenomenon."

Orfanides told Hazelwood that the police kept suggesting ways that he could have caused things to fly and typewriters to break down. At the same time, they assured him that he would probably not be prosecuted. At last, to end the incessant interrogation as quickly as possible, Orfanides had simply agreed with them.

"I told them I threw everything. I couldn't think of any other way it could be done."

Although the classic poltergeist formula usually has a young person present who is in the throes of puberty, it was pointed out by reporter Hazelwood that John Orfanides is emotionally high-strung and sensitive. He was upset to the point of illness that the police should even consider him guilty of the disturbances. It should also be noted that young Orfanides had been recently married. Poltergeists have been known to plague those making marital adjustments as well as those entering puberty.

Hazelwood is convinced of John Orfanides' innocence of being consciously responsible for the chaos in the Wheelers' office. In a letter dated July 30, 1965, Hazelwood told me: "I suspected him (Orfanides) almost from the first and would have loved to have been able to expose him as the trickster. It was just not possible to do so. At the same time, all activity ceased the moment Orfanides left the building. This happened on several occasions. . . . In fact, he was out of the room, but not the building, more often than not when the events occurred.

"I went into this as a hard-nosed reporter with almost 20 years in the business. I was prepared to scoff, expose, disbelieve. I came out of it absolutely convinced that the poltergeist phenomenon is a real one which cannot be explained by our present knowledge of natural laws."

THE DRUMMER OF TEDWORTH

THE WEIRD phenomena that beset the family of John Mompesson of Tedworth, England in March of 1661 had the bizarre overtones of witchcraft and the fixing of a terrible curse. In this respect, the case is similar to that of Shchapoff's dancing poltergeist, allegedly brought on by the curse of a miller's servant, and the stone-throwing devil that was supposedly set on George Walton by the widow whose lands he had obtained by nefarious means. The "demon" of Tedworth is so much a part of the legend and folklore of England that ballads and poems have been written in celebration of the incredible prowess of the poltergeist.

Of greatest help to the serious student of psychic phenomena, who wishes to sift fact from fancy, is the work, *Saducismus Triumphatus*, by the Reverend Joseph Glanvil. The Rev. Glanvil investigated and witnessed the phenomena while it was in progress, and in spite of observations which are colored by the man's times, he has left an extraordinary record of a violent poltergeist disturbance.

John Mompesson, a justice of the peace, had brought before him an ex-drummer in Cromwell's army, who had been demanding money of the Bailiff by virtue of a suspicious pass. The Bailiff had believed the pass to be counterfeit, and Mr. Mompesson, who was familiar with the handwriting of the gentlemen who had allegedly signed the note, immediately declared the paper to be a forgery.

The drummer, whose name was Drury, begged Mompesson to check his story with Colonel Ayliff of Gretenham. The Colonel would vouch for his integrity, the drummer insisted. Mompesson was swayed by the drummer's pleas that he not be put into jail, but he told the man that he would confiscate his drum until he had checked out his story. Drury demanded that his drum be returned, but Mompesson told him to be on his way and to give thanks for his own freedom.

Mompesson had the drum sent to his house for safekeeping, then left on a business trip to London. Upon his return, his wife informed him that the household had been terrorized by strange noises in the night. She could only accredit the sounds to burglars trying to break into the house. On the third night of his return, Mompesson was brought to his feet by a loud knocking that seemed to be coming from a side door. With a pistol in one hand and another in his belt, Mompesson opened the door. There was no one there, but now the knocking had begun at another door. He flung that one open, too, and finding no one there, walked around the outside of the house in search of the culprit. He found no one on his search, nor could he account for the hollow drumming that sounded on the roof when he went back to bed.

From that night on, the drumming came always just after the Mompessons had gone to bed. It made no difference whether they retired early or late, the invisible drummer was ever prepared to tap them a lullaby. After a month of being contented with rooftop maneuvers, the disturbances moved inside—into the room where Mompesson had placed the ex-soldier's drum. Once it had established itself in the home, the ghostly drummer favored the family with two hours of martial rolls, tattoos, and points of war each evening.

On the night in which Mrs. Mompesson was being delivered of a child, the drummer was respectfully quiet; it maintained this silence for a period of three weeks, as if it were allowing the mother to fully recover her strength before it began its pranks in earnest.

The children were the ones who suffered most when the drummer terminated its truce. With terrible violence, the thing began beating on their bedsteads at night. It would raise the children's beds in time with its incessant drumming, and, when it finally did quiet down, it would lay under their beds scratching at the floor. The Mompessons hopefully tried moving their children to another room, but it did no good. The drummer moved right along with them.

By November 5th, the drummer had achieved such strength that it could hand boards to a servant who was doing some repair work in the house. This was witnessed by a roomful of people, but Mompesson soon forbade his servant "such familiarities."

When the thing began to leave behind offensive, sulphurous fumes, the Mompessons took this as sufficient evidence that their unwelcome guest had come directly from the pit of Hades. A Reverend Cragg was summoned to conduct a prayer meeting in the house. The drummer maintained a reverent silence during the minister's prayers, but upon the last "amen," it began to move chairs about the room, hurl the children's shoes into the air, and toss every object that it could get its invisible hands on. A heavy staff struck Rev. Cragg on the leg, but the astonished clergyman reported that "a lock of wool could not have fallen more softly."

The knocking had become so loud at nights that it awakened neighbors several houses away. The Mompessons' servants had also become privileged to receive nocturnal visits from the drummer. Their beds were raised while they attempted sleep, and, at times "it would lie like a great weight about their feet."

It particularly delighted in wrestling with a husky servant named John. It would jerk the bedclothes off the sleeping man, throw shoes at his head, and engage in a hearty tug-o'-war with the man, who was trying desperately to keep the covers on his bed instead of on the floor. At times, the powerful poltergeist would entwine itself around John and "forcibly hold him as if he were bound hand and foot." With a tremendous effort of brute strength, the servant would free himself from the grasp of his invisible opponent and reach for the sword that he kept beside his bed. John had found that the brandishing of his sword was the only action that could make the thing retreat.

By January 10, 1662, nearly a year after its unwelcome arrival, the entity had acquired a voice and the ability to simulate the sound of rustling silk and the panting of animals. It had begun by singing in the chimney, then moved into the children's bedroom where it had chanted: "A witch, a witch, I am a witch!" When Mompesson rushed into the nursery with his pistol, the disturbances ceased at once.

That night it came to his bedside, panting like a large dog. The bedroom, even though lacking a fireplace, and on a particularly cold and bitter winter's night, became very hot and filled with a noxious odor.

On the following morning, Mompesson scattered fine ashes over the chamber floor to see what sort of imprints might be made by the incredible entity. He was rewarded—and puzzled—by the discovery of the markings of a great claw, some letters, circles, and other eerie "footprints."

It was at this point in the manifestations that Reverend Joseph Glanvil arrived to conduct his investigation. The phenomena were most co-operative for Rev. Glanvil and provided him with ample evidence of their existence from the very first moment of his arrival. It was eight o'clock in the evening and the children were in bed, enduring their nightly ritual of scratching, bed-liftings, and pantings. Rev. Glanvil tried desperately to trace the source of the disturbances, but could find nothing. He was momentarily elated when he noticed something moving in a linen bag, but upon scooping up the cloth, and hoping to find a rat or a mouse in his clutches, he was dismayed to find himself left holding an empty bag.

Later that night, when Rev. Glanvil and a friend retired for the evening, they were awakened by a loud knocking.

"What would you have to do with us?" the clergyman asked the entity.

"Nothing with you," a disembodied voice answered him.

The next morning, Rev. Glanvil's horse was found trembling in a state of nervous exhaustion.

"It looks as though the beast has been ridden all night," a puzzled servant said.

Glanvil had scarcely mounted the horse for his return trip when the animal collapsed. Although the horse was well attended and cared for, it died within two days.

One night in the children's bedroom, the voice shrieked its claim that it was a witch over a hundred times in rapid succession. The next day, the harried Mompesson fired his pistol at an animated stick of firewood and was astonished to see several drops of blood appear on the hearth! The firewood fell to the floor and a trail of blood began to drip on the stairway as the wounded drummer retreated. One wishes that a modern pathologist's laboratory could have had an opportunity to analyze the drops for blood-type.

When the thing returned three nights later, it seemed to vent its anger on the children. Even the baby was tormented and not allowed to sleep. At last, Mompesson arranged to have the children taken to the house of friends. At this tactic, the drummer pounded severely on Mompesson's bedroom door, then quitted its post there to show itself to a servant.

"I could not determine the exact proportion," the terrified man told his master, "but I saw a great body with two red and glaring eyes, which for some time were fixed steadily upon me."

When the children were returned to their home, the thing seemed to want to make up to them. The Mompessons and their servants could hear distinctly "a purring, like that of a cat" in the nursery. The contented purring, however, turned out to be but another ploy of the devilish drummer. Four hours later, it was beating the children's legs against the bedposts, and emptying chamber pots into their beds.

A friend, who had stayed the night in the house that had gone berserk, had all of his coins turned black. His unfortunate horse was discovered in the stables with one of its hind legs firmly fastened in its mouth. It took several men working with a lever to dislodge the hoof from the animal's jaws.

At about this time, Drury, the man whose drum Mompesson had confiscated, was located in Gloucester Gaol where he had been sentenced for thievery. Upon questioning, he freely admitted "witching" Tedworth's justice of the peace. "I have plagued him," the man boasted, "and he shall never be quiet 'till he hath made me satisfaction for taking away my drum!"

Mompesson had the drummer tried for witchcraft at Sarum, and the man was condemned to be transported to one of the English colonies. Certain stories have it that the man so terrified the ship's captain and crew by "raising storms" that they took him back to port and left him on the dock before sailing away again. While on board ship, he had told the captain that he had been given certain books of the Black Arts by an old wizard, who had tutored him in the finer points of witchcraft.

By the time a King's commission had arrived to investigate the alleged haunting, the phenomena had been quiet for several weeks. The cavaliers spent the night with the Mompessons, then left the next morning, declaring that the entire two-year haunting was either a hoax or the misinterpretation of natural phenomena by credulous and superstitious men.

Reverend Joseph Glanvil's frustration with His Majesty's investigators is obvious in the conclusion of *Saducismus Triumphatus*, where he writes: ". . .'twas bad logic to conclude in matters of fact from a single negative and such a one against numerous affirmatives, and so affirm that a thing was never done . . . By the same way of reasoning . . . the Spaniard inferred well that said 'There is no sun in England, because I was there for six weeks and never saw it.' This is the common argument of those that deny the being of apparitions. They have travelled all hours of the night and have never seen any thing worse than themselves (which may well be) and thence they conclude that all pretended apparitions are fancies or impostures."

Before we accept Drury's claim of magic powers, we must remember that witchcraft was a very real thing to the people of 1663. Poltergeistic phenomena was also a very real thing, but had not yet been given a name, nor had "noisy hauntings" been recognized as anything other than the work of Satan. Although it is difficult to determine exactly from Glanvil's report, John Mompesson must have had at least three children, excluding the baby that was born during the manifestations. Of these, one was at the age when the phenomenon seems to be most attracted to people, and another was approaching puberty. It is very likely that the "drummer" of Tedworth began quite independently of the bitter ex-soldier who claimed to have put a curse on John Mompesson. When Drury learned of the disturbances at Tedworth, it would not seem at all inconsistent with his character to conjecture that he might have taken the credit for originating the manifestations. On the other hand, one should again recognize the terribly potency which some people accredit to "curses" (the direction of negative suggestion) and consider the possibility that Drury's "witchcraft" may have been intensified by the frustrations and repressions of the pubertal Mompesson children.

PECKHAM'S PESKY POLTERGEIST

THE STRINGERS finally had to call the ghost "Larry" because their four-year-old son kept asking about the column of vibrating light.

"We had to give the child some sort of explanation," Graham Stringer said to a reporter for United Press International. "We didn't want to frighten him with a lot of ghost talk."

"Larry" would be benign most of the year, but each Easter season since 1958, the strange entity had brought mysterious fires to their home on Trafalgar Avenue in the Peckham district of London.

"It was on Good Friday of 1958 that we first saw the thing," Stringer said. It was a milky, fluorescent column of vibrating light about as tall as a man. Shortly after seeing the apparition, the Stringers smelled smoke coming from the baby's room.

"There we found that something had burned a hole through the center of a pile of the baby's clothes. It looked just as though a blowtorch had done it. Yet, a pair of nylons on the bottom of the pile was untouched—and you know how flammable they are."

In 1959, the Easter season once again brought "Larry" instead of the Easter Bunny. When Stringer had a pair of shoes yanked out of his hands, he decided that it was time to call in the experts. A team of investigators from the College of Psychic Science was not able to achieve a conclusive analysis of the disturbances, but they definitely identified the phenomenon as being poltergeistic in nature. Their series of psyche-probing questions also established the fact that Mrs. Stringer had experienced the visitation of a poltergeist during her adolesence. Mr. Stringer also recalled similar phenomena that had gone essentially unnoticed during their honeymoon.

Although the Stringers were prepared for "Larry" when he returned in 1960, they were powerless to prevent the murky column of light from burning up another pile of clothes.

Their annual weekend houseguest had decided to extend its stay a bit, too. Clocks were still moving about on the mantelpiece, and objects were still floating around the apartment for several days after Easter Sunday. Stringer, who is a free-lance photographer, also reported being enveloped in a gray, fluorescent cloud while working in his darkroom. "The room lit up," he told reporters. "And there was Larry vibrating at my side."

In 1961, the Stringers tried a little preventive exorcism with a Catholic priest administering the rites shortly before their annual visitor was due to arrive.

"It seemed to have done the trick," Stringer said, "and we congratulated ourselves all around."

The festivities were premature. "Larry" had simply taken a year's sabbatical. In 1962, the Stringers' living room furniture burst into flames. In addition to losing many pieces in the fire, the harrassed family also had their carpet and their son's bed consumed by flames that had erupted spontaneously.

On April 21, 1962, a medium, whom the Stringers had contacted, disclosed that "Larry" was in reality "Mrs. Stringer's brother, Charles, who had died from burns 20 years earlier at the age of 18 months."

"Now that the spirit has made his identity known," the medium announced, "he will leave the family in peace."

Whether "Larry" actually was Charles or whether the phenomenon was due to some long-repressed, subconsciously-nurtured guilt on the part of Mrs. Stringer, who may, as a child, have considered herself in some way

139

responsible for her brother's death, the Easter poltergeist has not returned to burn any more clothing in the
Stringer's home in Peckham.

A MOST UNUSUAL MAID

ON A Monday forenoon, January 6, 1772, Mrs. Golding
was startled to hear the crashing of china and glasses
come from the back kitchen of her home in Stockwell,
England.

Ann Robinson, her 20-year-old maid, appeared at the
door to the parlor. "The plates seem to be falling from
the shelf, Mrs. Golding."

Mrs. Golding rolled impatient eyes toward the ceiling. "That, my child, seems to be obvious. Now sweep
up the mess, and do be more careful, won't you?"

"But I didn't do it, Mrs. Golding," the girl insisted.
"There's something very peculiar going on. I think you'd
better come see."

Mrs. Golding raised herself from the chair with some
effort. She was no longer a young woman. She had
hired the Robinson girl so that she might be able to
spend more time sitting in her parlor than scurrying
about in the kitchen.

"See there?" the girl pointed to the broken china on
the floor. "They simply fell down from the shelf."

"No one can argue with that," Mrs. Golding nodded
her head wearily. "Now please clean up the fragments
before they become scattered all over the kitchen."

Mrs. Golding was turning to leave the kitchen when
a row of plates suddenly rolled off another shelf and
shattered on the floor.

"See!" the girl shouted. "I wasn't near that shelf."

Mrs. Golding raised a hand to calm her. "But you
must not have put the dishes away carefully when you
placed them on that shelf. You must learn to be more . . ."

Her lecture was interrupted by a series of crashes
that sounded from various rooms in the house. "Mercy
upon us!" she gasped. "Whatever is happening!"

With the young maid's help, Mrs. Golding made an
inspection of her cottage. A clock had tumbled down
and broken its case. A lantern that had hung on the

staircase had been smashed on the steps. Several pictures had fallen from their places and cracked the glass
in their frames. An earthenware pan of salted beef had
crumbled to pieces, and the beef scattered. Even as the
two women moved through the house, objects began
leaping from their places and to fall crashing to the
floor. The events were too much for Mrs. Golding. She
ran from her cottage into the home of Mr. Gresham,
a next door neighbor, and fainted.

Miss Robinson told Mr. Gresham of the strange situation that existed in the Golding house, and he called
Mr. Rowlidge, a carpenter, who had recently completed
some remodeling work in the cottage.

"It's as I told Mrs. Golding," Rowlidge said as he surveyed the chaos of her home, "the foundation simply
can't take the added weight of that room she had me add
on upstairs. The whole business is very apparent to me.
The foundation is crumbling under that additional
weight. Mrs. Golding's things must be moved at once
before the entire house collapses."

While Mrs. Golding rested in the home of Mr. Gresham, workmen set about moving her effects from the
home that the carpenter had declared was in imminent
danger. Ann Robinson busied herself with the packing
of trunks and boxes for the workmen to carry.

"That girl is a cool one," one of the workmen remarked.
"The house could collapse at any moment, and she's
upstairs packing, just as calm as you please."

Mr. Rowlidge finally insisted that Ann leave the
house. "I'm not afraid," she told the carpenter. "There's
really nothing to be afraid of."

In the meantime, Mrs. Pain, Mrs. Golding's niece,
had arrived from the farm at Brixton Causeway. Shocked
at her aunt's distraught condition, Mrs. Pain arranged
for Mr. Gardner, a surgeon, to bleed Mrs. Golding.
Blood-letting was, of course, the standard medical cure-
all of the day, and the surgeon asked that the blood be
kept in a basin so that he might examine it when it
cooled.

The blood had only just begun to congeal when it
gushed out of the basin onto the floor. The surgeon and
the others had barely finished exclaiming over the curious incident when the basin itself exploded. The nerv-

ous surgeon reached for a bottle of rum to steady his nerves, but before he could pour himself a shot, the decanter shattered in his hand.

At the same time, workmen, who had paused in their moving to uncork a bottle of wine, were angered when the bottle broke in pieces before they could pour out a single glassful.

Jars of pickles, bottles of liquors, and china began to leap out of the boxes that the workmen had carried into Mr. Gresham's house.

"It's certain that there is nothing wrong with *your* foundation, Mr. Gresham," Mrs. Golding remarked from the bed in which she was resting. "It seems quite apparent that some evil force is following me about. I shan't endanger your home any longer. I must move."

"You'll come home with me, Auntie," Mrs. Pain said. "You and Ann are welcome to stay at the farm with us."

Mrs. Golding accepted her niece's offer, and while Mrs. Pain set about making the necessary arrangements, the woman and her maid went to the home of Mr. Mayling, another neighbor. Here, gratefully, no disturbances followed them. At about two o'clock in the afternoon, Mrs. Pain arrived with a carriage to take the two women out to the farm at Rush Common, near Brixton Causeway.

It was not until eight o'clock that evening that the manifestations returned, and, once again, the first area of attack was the kitchen. An entire row of pewter dishes leaped, one by one, from a shelf to the middle of the floor. When they were picked up and placed on a living room dresser, the entire performance was repeated.

An egg flew off a shelf, crossed the room, and scored a direct hit on a cat that had been sleeping before the hearth.

Mary Martin, Mrs. Pain's servant, was not at all happy with the chaos that had come to her kitchen, but as she had once been Mrs. Golding's servant, she resolved to make the best of the situation—even when a heavy fireplace poker leaped into the air, narrowly missing her.

Candlesticks flew from their places on the mantle. A teapot struck Ann Robinson on the foot. A large china bowl sailed more than eight feet to land behind a sofa. Richard Fowler, a neighbor of the Pains, was astonished to see that the bowl had not received even the slightest chip. He carried it carefully back to its place in the middle of a table. Once there, it crumbled to pieces.

Fowler was asked to stay the night with the Pains and help maintain a kind of watch over the phenomena. The man lasted until one o'clock in the morning, then he left the farmhouse in terror.

Not a single room was safe from the disturbances. Furniture moved or collapsed; tumblers and plates sailed about the rooms; hams dropped off their hooks in the kitchen.

"What have we done to bring such an affliction upon us?" Mrs. Golding wondered aloud.

"Don't be alarmed, Mrs. Golding," Ann Robinson told her mistress. "These things can't be helped. They are common occurrences which must happen in every family.

Mrs. Golding was stunned to hear such advice coming from the servant girl. Everyone else was terrified by the disturbances, yet here was a 20-year-old girl advising everyone to remain calm and suggesting that nothing was really out of the ordinary at all. Now that she stopped to think about it, Mrs. Golding remembered that Ann had been remarkably cool about the manifestations from the very beginning. Could the girl, in some way, be responsible for the frightening acts?

"Doesn't that girl of yours ever sit down?" Mr. Pain's question intruded upon her thoughts.

"She's always on the move. She seems so calm about the whole business, yet her constant walking about betrays her nervousness."

Mrs. Golding realized that it was so. Ann Robinson's features remained composed, but she had been on her feet ever since they had arrived at the Pain's farm. The only time that she had really been quiet was when, after supper, the family had knelt together for five minutes of prayer. Then, Mrs. Golding reflected, the disturbances had been quiet, too.

By five o'clock on Tuesday morning, there was hardly a cup or saucer left unbroken in the Pains' cupboards. All the chairs, tables, dressers, and other movable pieces of furniture had been either damaged or dashed about the rooms of the farmhouse.

"I've got to leave this house," said Mrs. Golding, who had refused to go to bed that night. "I've got to leave before your home is completely destroyed."

"But where will you go, Auntie?" Mrs. Pain wondered. "We can't just turn you out."

Mrs. Golding expressed her thanks for her niece's thoughtfulness, but Mrs. Pain had not been able to hide her anguish when some of her favorite pieces of china had been dashed to the floor by the invisible agency which had attached itself to her aunt. Mrs. Golding realized that the bonds of kinship were so strong in Mrs. Pain that she would be welcome to stay at the farm until every dish had been shattered and every piece of furniture had been smashed into kindling. But Mrs. Golding could not, in all conscience, remain with her niece and permit such a thing to happen.

"Fowler will take you in until we can find a place for you," Mr. Pain said.

Mrs. Golding smiled. "The way he fled this house at one o'clock, I doubt very much if he'll want the evil spirits to move right in with him."

"Don't underestimate Fowler," Mr. Pain advised. "He's a brave enough man. Things just got a little too much for him last night."

As Pain suggested, his neighbor extended his hospitality to the poor old woman and her young maid. He had hardly settled them in a room, however, when a lantern jumped off its hook and spilled its oil on the floor. A candlestick and a lamp became airborne at the same time, circled in the air, and crashed into one another in mid-flight. To cover his fright, Richard Fowler retreated into the kitchen, where a basket of coal tipped over and sent lumps of coal jumping along the floor as if they were black toads.

Ann Robinson had followed the frightened man into the kitchen. "If you allow my mistress to stay," she told him, "such things will continue to happen in your house, and worse things may follow."

Fowler approached Mrs. Golding in the room to which he had just shown her and begged her to leave his house at once. He apologized for reneging on his

144

hospitality, but added: "It seems to me, dear lady, that Providence is determined to punish you on this side of the grave for some terrible sin that you must have committed. Search your soul and try to make amends, for it seems that Providence is trying to make an object lesson out of you."

Mrs. Golding could not blame Richard Fowler for wanting her to leave his home, but she was extremely upset that she, a woman of excellent reputation, should be accused of harboring some secret sin.

The beleagured woman sent for Mr. Pain and asked him to take her and Ann Robinson back to her own house in Stockwell. "I'll not bring grief to anyone else's home," she told Pain. "And if I truly am being punished for some sin, I may just as well await Divine Justice in my own home."

Neighbors reported that there had been no disturbances in the house since Mrs. Golding and her maid had left the day before at two o'clock in the afternoon. Mr. Rowlidge, the carpenter, had come to revise his theory of a crumbling foundation and had decreed the house perfectly safe.

The moment that the two women stepped inside the door, however, things began to happen. A nine-gallon cask of beer turned itself upside down. A pail of water that had been left on the kitchen floor began to boil like a pot over a flame. A heavy mahogany table, that had been left by the workmen because of its great size, upset itself in the parlor.

Mrs. Golding swooned into the arms of Mr. Pain. She was an old woman and the excitement was becoming far too much for her.

"Quickly, Ann," Pain told the maid, "take the carriage and go fetch Mrs. Pain."

The servant girl did as she was told, and Mr. Pain was not at all surprised when the disturbances ceased the instant that she had left the house. He had been doing some thinking of his own. He, too, had been intrigued by the girl's strange coolness in the midst of such incredible phenomena, and he had soon noticed that the manifestations were quiet whenever she left the building for any reason. He explained his theory to Mrs. Golding, and she quickly added her own observations. Somehow, they agreed, Ann Robinson was responsible for the fantastic series of events that had begun twenty-four hours earlier. Their theory received all the proof it needed when the manifestations began again the moment that Ann returned with Mrs. Pain.

"I'm sorry, Ann," Mrs. Golding told her, "but I must discharge you."

The servant girl accepted her dismissal with the same lack of emotion with which she had weathered the violence of the phenomena. She went quickly to her room, packed her things, and left, taking with her the energy center of the rambunctious poltergeist.

It is a pity that we don't know more about Ann Robinson. It would indeed be interesting to determine whether or not she had somehow been able to set a poltergeist in action by malicious intent, or if she regarded herself innocent of any conscious part in the disturbances and also believed that Mrs. Golding was receiving punishment for some scandal in her past.

THE TERRIBLE ROOM AT WILLINGTON MILL

FOR TWO MONTHS the nursemaid had tried to ignore the strange noises that she had heard coming from the deserted room over the nursery. The sounds came each night when she was left alone to watch the child—a dull, heavy tread, like someone slowly pacing back and forth.

For eight weeks she had chosen to ignore the sounds, but now, she announced to her employer, Mr. Joseph Proctor, she was asking to be discharged from his service. "I am persuaded that it is something supernatural up there, and it has quite upset me," she told him.

As the woman was obviously in a state of great nervous agitation, Proctor saw no reason why he should attempt to talk her into staying with them. It wasn't long, however, before he too heard the sound of heavy feet in the upstairs room, as did his wife and the other servants. Although puzzled by the eerie tread of invisible feet, the Proctors convinced themselves that there was undoubtedly some natural explanation for the phenomenon.

In spite of their refusal to take the noises seriously,

they purposely omitted any mention of the disturbed room when they hired a new nursemaid on January 23, 1835. On her first evening in the nursery, the girl came down to the sitting room to inquire who was in the room above her. The Proctors evaded her questions, putting the whole matter down to "just the usual night noises in an old house."

The next day, Mrs. Proctor heard the steps of a man with heavy boots walking about in the upstairs room. That same day, while the family was at dinner, the nursemaid came down the stairs and blinked incredulously at Mr. Proctor. "I've been hearing someone walking in the room above me for five minutes," she told him. "I had come down to assure myself that it wasn't you, sir. But if it isn't you, who is it?"

Proctor inspected the room that night. Trickery seemed out of the question. The empty room was covered with a thin, undisturbed layer of soot, which in itself was proof that not even a mouse had been walking about on the floor. The window had been boarded up many years ago with wooden laths and plaster, and the door to the room had been nailed shut for some time. Proctor descended even more mystified then when he had gone up to conduct his investigation.

On the 31st, the Proctors heard a dozen loud thuds sound next to their bed as they were preparing to retire. On the next night, Joseph Proctor heard a metallic rapping on the baby's crib. There was a brief pacing over head, and then the sound of footsteps, which were never heard again in the upper room.

But what followed for the next several years included such visible and auditory manifestations that the plodding footsteps were to seem like a baby's first steps in comparison. What is nearly as remarkable as the intense "haunting" of Willington Mill is the fact that the Proctors persisted in living in the house for over eleven years before finally surrendering to some of the most eerie paranormal disturbances on record.

Thomas Mann, the foreman of the mill that was separated from the Proctor's house by a road and a garden, told Proctor that he had heard a peculiar noise moving across the lawn in the darkness. At first, Mann thought it came from the wooden cistern that stood in the mill yard, and he suspected that some pranksters were making off with it. Upon pursuing the noise with a lantern in hand, Mann had found nothing; and the cistern, he later testified, had not been budged. Mann also told Proctor in the strictest confidence that he had been hearing a sound like invisible steps on the gravel walk.

It was shortly after their confidential conversation that both Mann and another neighbor observed the luminous phantasm of a woman in a window of Proctor's house. Both parties had seen the apparition independent of each other, and Mann had called his entire family to witness the phantasm, which was fully visible for over ten minutes.

About a year after the phenomena were in full swing, Jane Carr, Mrs. Proctor's sister, arrived for a stay at the mill. A few minutes before midnight, she was awakened by a noise very much like that of someone winding a large clock. After this "signal noise," her bed began to shake and she clearly heard a sound like that of a heavy sack falling on the floor above. Several strong knocks sounded about her bedstead, and the unmistakable shuffle of feet surrounded her bed.

One night, the phenomena specialized in bed-lifting. It manifested itself under the older child's crib (the disturbances had not prevented the Proctors from producing a family) by raising the mattress until he cried out, then it hoisted the mattress of the bed on which Mrs. Proctor and a new nursemaid were sleeping. Mrs. Proctor described the sensation as feeling "as if a man were underneath pushing it up with his back."

In addition to feet, the poltergeist had soon acquired invisible hands with which to pound on walls and lift beds. These achievements would seem as child's play, however, as the thing began to develop its ability to whistle and talk and materialize itself into a number of grotesque phantoms.

The boys, Joseph and Henry, were awakened one night by a loud shriek, which had sounded from under their cribs. Joseph, Sr., upon investigating, heard an eerie moan coming from somewhere in the room. A bed began to move and the voice spoke its first words—or what sounded like the words, "chuck-chuck." These sounds were followed by a noise similar to that of a child sucking at a bottle. The youngest child, Jane, was moved to another room, but she was not spared the torment of having her bed levitated.

The phenomena had begun to leave its domain on the upper floor and go on foraging expeditions during the night. As is so often the case in poltergeist phenomena, the kitchen seemed to be a favorite target for its nightly forays. The cook would, on several mornings, find the kitchen chairs heaped in a disorderly pile, the shutters thrown open, and utensils scattered about the room.

Mrs. Proctor's brother, Jonathan Carr, spent a night filled with bed-shakings and whistlings and declared that he would not live in the house for any amount of money.

Jane Carr, Mrs. Proctor's sister, was much more strong-nerved than her brother, and judging from Proctor's journal, the young woman spent many nights in the afflicted house. One night as she lay sleeping with the cook, Mary Young, the two women were terrified to hear the bolt in their door slide back, the handle turn, and the door open. Something rustled the curtains as it moved across the bed, then it lifted the bedclothes from the trembling figures. As it passed around the bed to Mary's side, both women distinctly saw a dark shadow against the curtain.

Little Jane Proctor was sleeping with her aunt Jane one night when she saw a strange head peeping out at her from the curtains at the foot of the bed. The four-year-old girl later described the head as being that of an old woman, but she became much too frightened to continue her observation and tucked her own head under the covers.

Joseph Jr., was disturbed nearly every night by some facet or other of the phenomena. He reported hearing the words, "Never mind" and "Come and get" being repeated over and over without any meaningful application. Footsteps were constantly parading around his bed, and thumpings sounded about his pillow and other bedclothes.

A Doctor Drury arrived and asked Proctor's permission to carry out an examination of the haunted upper room. Proctor consented and allowed the doctor and his companion, a young chemist, to make preparations to spend the night in the disturbed room. At about one o'clock in the morning, Proctor was awakened by a ghastly shriek of terror coming from the upper floor. Dr. Drury had come face to face with the spectre of the wizened old woman. The two "ghost-hunters" spent the rest of the dark hours drinking coffee in the kitchen. They left the house at dawn. Proctor noted in his diary that the doctor had got "a shock that he will not soon cast off."

One of the most incredible materializations of the Willington Mill poltergeist was that of a monkey. Eight-year-old Joseph was seated atop a chest of drawers pretending that he was making a speech to the other children. Suddenly, in full view of all the children, including two-year-old Edmund (the third child that had been added to the family since the onset of the disturbances), a monkey appeared and began to tug at Joseph's shoe strap.

By the time Joseph Sr., came running in response to their excited cries, the children were scurrying about the floor, trying desperately to play with the mischievous monkey. Two-year-old Edmund was looking under chairs until his bedtime, trying to locate the "funny cat."

Years later, the memory of that incident was still vivid in Edmund Proctor's mind. In the December, 1892 issue of the *Journal of the Society for Psychical Research,* he wrote: "Now it so happens that this monkey is the first incident in the lugubrious hauntings, or whatever they may be termed, of which I have any recollection. I suppose it was, or might easily be, the first monkey that I had ever seen, which may explain my memory being so impressed that I have not forgotten it. A monkey, and, upstairs in the nursery, that is the business. My parents have told me that no monkey was known to be owned in the neighborhood, and that after diligent inquiry no organman or hurdy-gurdy boy, either with or without a monkey, had been seen anywhere about the place or neighborhood, either on that day or for a length of time . . . I have an absolutely distinct recollection of that monkey, and of running to see where it went to as it hopped out of the room and into

150

the adjoining Blue-room. We saw it go under the bed in that room, but it could not be traced or found anywhere afterwards. We hunted and ferretted about that room, and every corner of the house, but no monkey, or any trace of one, was more to be found."

The white face of what appeared to be an old woman was seen more and more often, but Joseph Jr., soon added an old man to the list of materializations. Aunt Jane Carr did not see the monkey, but she reported that she had heard the "sound of an animal leaping down off the easy chair."

Another astonishing bit of ultra-sophisticated materialization took place when the entity fashioned a double of Joseph, beneath his bed, but imagine his shock upon discovering his mirror-image hiding from him in the shadows. The boy was, at this time, about ten years old so his powers of observation must be given some credence. Besides, having grown up in a most extraordinary home, he was inured to the average run-of-the-mill haunting. Joseph, Jr., said that his spectral self-image, which was even dressed in a manner identical to his, walked back and forth between the window and the wardrobe before it gradually dematerialized.

Shortly after this dramatic episode, the Proctors' decided that they had endured enough. Patient Quakers though they were, eleven years of living amidst incessant psychic disturbances had been enough for them. They had also become fearful of "an unhappy effect, if not a permanent injury on the minds of their children should they remain longer in such a plague-ridden dwelling."

Proctor obtained a residence at Camp Villa, North Shields, and after assisting with the packing, sent the servants and the children on ahead. The last night Mr. and Mrs. Proctor spent alone in Willington Mill was perhaps the most frightening of all.

Throughout the night they lay and listened to "boxes apparently being dragged with heavy thuds down the now carpetless stairs, non-human footsteps stumped on the floors . . . and impossible furniture . . . dragged hither and thither by inscrutable agency; in short, a pantomimic or spiritualistic repetition of all the noises incident to a household flitting."

One dreadful thought kept running throught the Proctors' minds: the ghosts were packing to move along with them!

It was with indescribable relief that the Proctors arrived at the new residence to find it completely free of the former taint that had blemished eleven years of their lives. Their residency in the new home was blissfully untroubled by knockings, whistlings, footsteps, and phantasms.

THE CURIOUS COFFINS AT ARENSBURG

THE ECCLESIASTICAL court, which assembled periodically at Arensburg, on the island of Oesel in the Baltic, was stunned by the complaint which had been addressed to it.

"What are we to make of this?" a member of the Consistory asked his fellows. "The people complain that a mysterious force from one of the private chapels in the cemetery is killing their horses!"

The first complaint had been registered on June 22, 1844, by a peasant woman, who had driven to the cemetery for one of her regular visits to her mother's grave. Her horse had been tethered near the Buxhoewden chapel. The animal had allowed her only a few moments at the graveside before it began to shriek in terror. By the time she had reached the animal, it had collapsed in a wild-eyed frenzy and was frothing at the mouth. The woman had run for a veterinarian, who managed to save the horse by bleeding it.

On the following Sunday, several people had hitched their horses near the Buxhoewden chapel while they attended services in the church. When they had returned to their animals after mass, they were shocked to find their horses trembling in terror. Some people had claimed that they could hear weird rumbles and groans coming from within the Buxhoewden chapel. On the next Sunday, services had been interrupted by the loud stampings and snortings of eleven horses which had been tied near the same chapel. As the owners left the church in alarm, they had been startled to find several of the animals struggling on the ground in various stages of nervous collapse. Bleeding had been immediately prescribed as treatment, but the veterinarian was too late to save four of the horses. Again, several people insisted that they had heard eerie moanings issuing from within the Buxhoewden chapel.

The Consistory chose to ignore the complaints of the people for the time being. Perhaps the horses had eaten some noxious plants. Perhaps there was an outbreak of some new disease. The mysterious death of the horses was obviously a matter for a practitioner of veterinary medicine and could not in any way be considered the business of an ecclesiastical court.

The strange happenings in and around the Buxhoewden chapel became impossible to ignore, however, just a few days after the Consistory had dismissed. During a funeral service in the chapel, the assembled mourners were horrified to hear terrible groans coming from the vault below. After the service had been concluded, some of the stouter hearts went down to the vault to prepare for the interment of the latest coffin. They were quite unprepared for the sight that greeted them when they unlocked the heavy vault door and pushed it open. Nearly all of the coffins in the Buxhoewden vault had been removed from their resting places and had been heaped in a disorderly pile.

It seemed impossible to account for such a disrespectful act. No one had the key to the vault but a representative of the Buxhoewden family—the same man who now stood incredulously surveying the havoc that had been done to his family's final resting place.

"Who could have done such a terrible thing?" he said to the men who had accompanied him down into the vault. They quickly replaced the coffins in their proper order and made ready for the placing of the latest coffin.

Although the Buxhoewden family tried to squelch the spreading of rumors, it wasn't long before the tale had reached the ears of the members of the Consistory, and the ecclesiastical court felt obliged to make an official inquiry.

"We wish to perpetuate no scandal," a representative of the Buxhoewdens told the Baron de Guldenstubbe, who was President of the Consistory. "It seems apparent to us that some enemy of our family has managed to find a way into the vault in order to commit these senseless acts of desecration."

"It would seem impossible to enter the vault without a key," the Baron pointed out, "and only you have the key that opens the door to the vault. There may be more to this matter than meets the eye."

At last the Baron convinced two members of the Buxhoewden family to accompany him on an inspection of the vault. All three men gasped in shock when they found the coffins once again strewn about the underground vault.

"This settles the matter," Baron de Guldenstubbe told the Buxhoewdens. "You must consent to an official investigation."

A committee of eight was formed, including Baron de Guldenstubbe, the bishop of the province, two other members of the Consistory, a physician, the burgomaster, one of the syndics, and a secretary. Their first act was to examine the vault thoroughly. They were hardly surprised when they unlocked the vault to find the coffins again in a state of disarray.

The Baron de Guldenstubbe gave the order to open two or three of the coffins to determine whether or not robbery had been sufficient enough motive to tempt some "lewd fellow of the baser sort" into committing this awful act of desecration. The order was carried out, and all rings, jewelry, and other personal effects buried with the corpses were found to be still interred with their earthly possessors.

Next the Baron speculated that someone "seduced by the craft and malice of the Devil" might have dug a tunnel into the crypt for the sole purpose of terrorizing the village. Workmen took up a section of the floor, the foundations were tested, and the walls sounded, but no evidence of any tunnelling could be discovered.

The committee considered itself baffled for the time being. Perhaps whatever had caused the disturbance had passed over and would simply become a topic for a winter evening's story-telling session around a blazing fireplace. But the Baron insisted upon an official test of the phenomenon.

After the coffins had been replaced, fine wood-ashes were scattered over the floor of the vault. The committee

154

then sealed the door with both Consistory and municipal seals and scattered ashes over the stairs leading from the vault to the chapel. As an added precaution against anyone gaining unlawful admittance into the crypt, armed guards would maintain a 24-hour-a-day watch for three days and nights to prevent any person from even approaching the building.

"It is now humanly impossible for anyone to gain entrance into the vault," the Baron proclaimed.

At the end of the three-day testing period, the committee returned and ordered the guards to open the vault. The seals remained unbroken until the guards swung the huge door on its hinges. The coating of ashes on the stairs leading down to the vault had betrayed no imprint of either man or animal.

The committee could only utter exclamations of frustration and wonder when their sputtering torches revealed the coffins of the Buxhoewdens in an even worse state than before. This time, many of the coffins had been set on end; and one coffin (that of a suicide) had had its lid opened. It was as if the strange force responsible for the disturbances had felt compelled to put on an extra exhibition of its abilities for such an illustrious group of gentlemen as the committee from the Consistory.

The Baron de Guldenstubbe made out an official report, and each of the committee members signed as witnesses. To the committee, the curious occurrences in the Buxhoewden chapel were totally inexplicable. We may, in conclusion, only repeat what has been suggested in earlier chapters. It seems quite possible, in the light of such cases as the moving coffins at Arensburg—and the equally curious crypt at Barbados—that poltergeist phenomena may be fed by an intelligence or a memory pattern which survives death, as well as from pubertal change or sexual shock in the living.

THE HEP POLTERGEIST THAT DUG ROCK AND ROLL

THE REV. JOHN JOHNSTONE, vicar of Ashton Keynes, was understandably surprised when he was called in to exorcise a ghost "that danced and beat time to rock and roll music."

The request for an exorcist came from a woman who lived in a house trailer with her 13-year-old son at Leigh, near Chicklade, Wiltshire, England. "Whenever the boys sings along with those terrible records," the woman reported, "the trailer begins to dance and dishes and things begin to sail through the air."

The Reverend Johnstone learned that the phenomena in the trailer had begun after the roof was removed from a near-by 200-year-old cottage which had a reputation for being haunted. It seemed impossible to tell whether the ancient ghost was acknowledging its approval of such contemporary classics as "I Want to Hold Your Hand," or if it was being critical of such modern musical abuses and was trying to put in its request for "My Lady Greensleeves."

The clergyman reported that he could "feel the spirit's vibrations the moment that I entered the trailer late on a Sunday evening to perform the rites of exorcism."

He asked the boy to sing a popular song, and almost at once the trailer began to rock in rhythm with the hand-slapping beat. A cup disengaged itself from the table and smashed against a wall.

Then the Reverend Johnstone requested that the boy sing a hymn. The teen-ager obliged, and the rocking of the trailer began to quiet down. No objects joined the flight pattern of the broken cup. He adjured the poltergeist to "quit this home and leave this woman in peace." At these words, the clergyman noted, the vibrations ceased."

Evidently the poltergeist was just being respectful toward a man of the cloth and his ritual. The woman testified that the manifestations began again immediately after the Reverend Johnstone had left their trailer. As they had done almost every evening since the poltergeist had moved in with them, they left their trailer to spend the night with friends.

When the Reverend Johnstone was informed that the poltergeist had only been playing possum for him, he told reporters that the woman and her son would either have to change trailer sites or the boy's taste in music.

THE INVISIBLE ARTIST

ON SUNDAY, March 10, 1850, Reverend Eliakim Phelps, a Presbyterian minister, and his family returned home from worship to find their furniture in a state of curious disarray. Hastening into the living room, the astonished family found the most amazing disturbance of all. There, in a sort of tableau, were eleven bizarre figures that had been constructed of articles of the family's clothing.

The strange dummies had been arranged in life-like attitudes of worship. Some were prostrate, their foreheads touching the floor. Others knelt about the room with open Bibles propped up before them. All of the figures were of females except for a grotesquely misshapen dwarf that stood in the center of the incredible scene.

The work of the invisible artist continued for about 18 months and was witnessed by a great many individuals of sound reputation. The phenomenon was also extensively reported in such newspapers as The New Haven *Journal Courier*. Such unusual events would create a sensation in any community, but in sedate little Stratford, Connecticut in 1850, the phenomenon could only be regarded as the handiwork of some extremely active spirits.

Poltergeist activity had not yet been named and classified, but a Mr. Andrew Jackson Davis, who personally investigated the disturbances, came close when he reported the phenomenon was due to "vital radiations that come from the elder (eleven-year-old) boy's organism and seem to be aided by magnetism from the elder girl (sixteen years old)." Mr. Davis also concluded, however, that there were spirits at work in the house.

The rooms were watched closely and steadily, but the artistic poltergeist continued to indulge its penchant for creative expression. The clothing which the invisible artist used for the figures was mysteriously gathered from the members of the Phelps family. Even the strictest sort of guard could not seem to deter the entity from collecting the necessary raw materials to create new tableaux. There were, it seemed, sufficient children

157

in the Phelps family (two girls and two boys) to supply the poltergeist with not only enough clothing, but also with enough psychic energy to keep itself working.

A Dr. Webster, who witnessed the phenomenon, wrote: "In a short space of time so many figures were constructed that it would not have been possible for half a dozen women, working steadily for several hours, to have completed their design and arranged the picturesque tableaux. Yet these things happened in a short space of time with the whole house on watch. Some (of the figures) were so life-like that, a small child being shown the room, thought his mother was kneeling in prayer with the rest."

Other phenomena soon gave evidence that the invisible artist could be destructive as well as creative. Dr. Webster said: "Objects of all kinds were thrown about the house by what seemed to be invisible hands. Window panes were broken and great damage was done to the walls and furnishings of the home. Rappings were constantly heard and these sometimes gave intelligent and blasphemous answers to questions that were asked."

Once while at his writing desk, Dr. Phelps was astonished to find that a previously blank piece of paper had become completely covered with strange, unintelligible writing. Another eye witness reported seeing the elder boy "carried across the room by invisible hands and deposited gently on the floor."

A reporter for the New Haven *Journal-Courier* told his incredulous readers that he had been summoned to the elder girl's room by the frightened child's screaming. The girl complained that she had been struck several times in rapid succession; and there was, indeed, an angry red mark on her cheek. As he attempted to comfort her, he was startled to see a large porcelain jug rise into the air, circle the room, then smash itself to the floor.

A system of communication that had been worked out with the "spirit" rappings informed the Rev. Phelps that it was the ghost of a French clerk, who had been employed by the firm of lawyers that had handled a settlement for his wife. The "spirit" claimed that it was being tormented in hell for cheating in the drawings up of the settlement papers. The minister was intrigued enough by the spirit messages to investigate the other-worldly claims. To his amazement, he learned that there had been a fraud perpetrated in the settlement and that the firm's French clerk had died only a few months previous to the onset of the phenomena in the Phelps' home. The clerk had only been guilty of a minor indiscretion, however, which seemed to the minister hardly deserving of such torment. And what bizarre scheme of justice, he pondered, sent the sinner back to haunt the sinned-against?

Dr. Phelps wasn't entirely sold on the returning-spirit hypothesis, and he is quoted in an interview as saying: "I am satisfied that the spirit communications are wholly worthless in that they are frequently false, contradictory and nonsensical . . . I place no value in any message, and if they are from spirits, they are from evil spirits."

In the same interview, Dr. Phelps was firm to declare the absence of duplicity on the part of any of his family: "The facts of the phenomena are such, and have transpired under such circumstances as to render the idea of tricks or design and deception wholly inadmissable. The reports in the newspapers have promulgated the idea that these are merely the tricks of children; but on many occasions the conditions have been such that there could have been no tricks by children or others."

A reporter for the New York *Sun* recorded that he was present when one of the daughters had her arm pinched by the invisible entity until the abused area was black and blue.

A Mr. H. B. Taylor swore that he was an eye-witness to an animated candlestick that beat itself against the floor until it was broken. He also claimed to have seen a shovel and fire-tong hop about in the middle of the floor, and a lamp move across the room to set fire to a pile of papers.

On October 1, 1851, the invisible artist left the Phelps family to express itself elsewhere. The minister's family had tolerated its tableaux and its acts of terrorism for eighteen months; they could hardly be considered a good audience any longer.

ACKNOWLEDGMENTS

THE AUTHOR MUST gratefully acknowledge the cooperation and the assistance tendered him by many individuals. Chief among these would be Dr. Arthur Hastings, Stanford University, Stanford, California; Dr. Stanley Krippner, Director of Research, Department of Psychiatry, Maimonides Hospital of Brooklyn; Mr. James Shaffer, staff writer and photographer, *Dubuque Telegraph Herald*, Dubuque, Iowa; Mr. James Hazelwood, Editorial Department, *Oakland Tribune*, Oakland, California, and Miss Ann McDonough of Edgewood, Iowa, for permission to explore the scrapbooks and files of her late brother, John. A special thank-you must be warmly directed to Mr. Ivan T. Sanderson for his many kindnesses, his continued encouragement, and his faith in my ability throughout the lengthy campaign of assembling and writing this book.

AFTERWORD
How Strange Guests came to be written

In 1963, after six years of teaching high school English and writing on weekends and holidays, I believed that I had sold enough short stories and articles to be able soon to realize my dream of becoming a full-time freelance writer. I accepted a position advising student publications and teaching creative writing at a small Iowa college, and I rented a room in a downtown office building where I could write off campus.

In 1965, I began writing "A Walk on the Weird Side," a weekly column for the Chicago-based tabloid *The National Tattler*. The column had only appeared for a couple of months when I received a "fan letter" from one of my heroes, Ivan T. Sanderson. I read the letter again and again. An author who I had admired for years had praised my writing style, my dedication to accuracy, and my knowledge of the paranormal field.

Neither my wife nor any of my friends could understand how thrilling it was to me to have received a complimentary letter from Sanderson. I tried to explain that it would be like a young soprano in a college choir receiving a complimentary note from Maria Callas, like a young pianist in a community orchestra receiving praise from Van Cliburn, like a young actor in summer stock receiving a good word from Marlon Brando. But no one really understood.

I began an immediate correspondence with Ivan. After a brief exchange, he informed me that he was an acquisitions editor for Chilton publishing and that he was looking for someone who could do a smashingly good job writing a book on poltergeist phenomena. He was convinced that I was just the author for whom he had been searching.

When I looked up Chilton in a writer's guide, I was puzzled to see that they were (and still are) noted primarily for their automotive publications, but I didn't question Ivan. If anyone could convince a publishing company famous for their automotive reference works to publish a book on poltergeists, it would be Ivan T. Sanderson.

Ivan sent me a sample presentation, which I found very helpful and informative. I had already written enough articles to have them collected in book form, *Ghosts, Ghouls, and Other Peculiar People*, and I had done the text for two photo books, *Monsters, Maidens and Mayhem: A Pictorial History of the Monster Movie* and *Master Movie Monsters*, but I had not really sold a publisher on a conventional book.

Ivan was enthusiastic about my presentation, and I set to work in earnest, expecting a contract and an advance to be soon on its way to me. Excitedly, I telephoned my parents and said that I was going to write a hardcover book on poltergeists. I didn't learn until months later that my mother had proudly told all of her friends that her farmer-boy son was writing a book on "poultry lice."

I never understood what happened next, but suddenly Ivan was no longer associated with Chilton. He encouraged me to keep working on the project in the hope that some day some publisher might be interested in it.

Ivan and I maintained a regular correspondence, and I continued to write articles on the paranormal, as well as features on current Hollywood productions and nostalgic pieces about legendary stars of the past. I also wrote short stories for *Alfred Hitchcock's Mystery Magazine*, *The Saint*, *Trapped*, *Fantastic*, and a number of men's magazines. Through a friend in Mystery Writers of America, I acquired a New York agent who sold Macfadden-Bartell, a major publisher in those days, the idea of my writing a biography of Rudolph Valentino, together with Chaw Mank, who had once headed The Great Lover's fan club. Irving Shulman's biography of Hollywood sex goddess Jean Harlow was the current cause célèbre of the publishing world, so, my agent asked, why not a "intimate biography" of Hollywood's first sex symbol?

Macfadden-Bartell brought me to New York for two weeks in January 1966 to complete work on *Valentino*. I was put up in a small suite at the Iroquois Hotel, the little sister of the legendary mecca of literary lore, the Algonquin. This was a very heady experience for a farm boy from Iowa, just one month shy of his thirtieth birthday, who, for as long as he could remember, had aspired to come to New York City and be a writer. During the days and nights in New York, I met with editors and writer friends and visited the offices of the magazines that had been publishing my articles and short stories.

And, of course, I took advantage of the proximity to the Sandersons' home outside of Blairstown, New Jersey, and I arranged to spend a weekend with them. Alma, Ivan's wife, was staying in their apartment in the city, so I had dinner with her on Thursday night and we traveled together to their country home on Friday afternoon.

When we arrived at the farm, Ivan greeted me warmly and ushered me into a large and comfortable guest room. I was amused to find that throughout the house there were stuffed chipmunks and other small mammals posed with placards in their paws proclaiming such endearments as "Ivan is a swine."

The walls held a number of beautiful photographs of the youthful Ivan and Alma on a variety of expeditions. Several taken aboard a sailing vessel seemed to be the very essence of romantic adventure. The exotic and lovely Alma in her sarong standing next to her handsome Scots husband reminded me of a South Seas movie with Dorothy Lamour and Ray Milland. As I recall, Ivan told me that they had met at his cousin's wedding in Paris and it had been love at first sight for the two of them.

As I had expected, Ivan was a great and courteous host and a marvelous raconteur at the dinner table. A number of times during the meal, Alma interrupted one of his lengthy discourses to remind him that we were his dinner companions, not members of a lecture audience.

After dinner, Ivan excitedly brought forth a special prize that he had been saving for me: a photograph of an actual poltergeist.

Alma dismissed the photograph of an adolescent girl standing near a water pump only as proof of Ivan's "insane obsession with the subject of poltergeists." As his wife of thirty years, she could get by with such a blunt analysis of Ivan's pet evidence of a psychokinetic entity.

I studied the picture carefully. Over the left shoulder of the girl was a slight blur, which Ivan declared was the psychic energy of the poltergeist that had been afflicting her family. I glanced up at Ivan, who was eagerly awaiting my agreement that the photograph had most certainly captured the essence of a poltergeist.

Ivan was once one of my idols who now, over several months of correspondence, had become a good friend. What could I say? I saw only the same blur that Alma saw.

"I suppose it's possible," I managed, as Alma arched an eyebrow and rolled her eyes in dismay at my cowardice in avoiding an outright contradiction of her husband's photographic evidence of a poltergeist. "It could be some kind of energy manifestation, I suppose. I mean, it is possible that the camera could capture a force that the eye could not see."

"It's more than possible," Ivan snorted, clearly not at all satisfied with my attempt at diplomacy. "That's exactly what it is – evidence of poltergeist energy."

Fortunately at this point, a number of the other dinner guests wanted to have a group discussion about the possibility of creating a newsletter for their newly formed Society for the Investigation of the Unexplained. I won't attempt to name all those assembled there at the Sandersons' that evening, but I was familiar with the bylines and the reputations of most of them.

By Saturday noon, many of the other house guests had departed, so I was able to spend the afternoon speaking with Ivan alone in his office and discussing subjects of special interest to each of us – from Yeti to poltergeists. He generously allowed me to copy a number of items from his monster, big snake, and poltergeist files.

As night fell, the telephone began to ring ceaselessly. "Damned Jersey Devil is running amok tonight," Ivan told me.

On a very cold Sunday morning with a light January snow falling, Ivan drove me into Blairstown to catch the train back to the city. I will always remember Ivan striding sockless through the snow in loafers, his open overcoat flapping in the wind at his sides as if he were a great Scots Thunderbird, impervious to inclement weather. I always tried to recall this image of Ivan the Invincible in later years when, during my trips to New York City, our visits together consisted mainly of my picking up his prescriptions at a neighborhood pharmacy and sitting at his bedside as he stoically attempted to ignore his illness and speak enthusiastically about his latest theories regarding UFOs, the Philadelphia experiment, the men-in-black, and sea monsters.

As work on *Valentino* was nearing completion, I had the great good fortune of meeting Evelyn Grippo, the editor of Ace Books. In 1966, Ace was doing extremely well with Frank Edwards and his "stranger than" paperbacks. When I discussed the poltergeist book with Evelyn, she expressed great interest with one proviso: the book must be presented in numerous brief chapters in order to follow the successful format established by the Edwards books.

This requirement did not seem unreasonable. Ivan had advised a book of 18 to 20 chapters, citing some data which claimed that readers preferred an even number of chapters. While I had grouped "categories" or "different kinds" of poltergeist activity into 18 chapters, it wouldn't be difficult to make subchapters into chapters.

After it appeared that Ace would definitely publish the poltergeist book, I called Ivan and he said that he would be more than pleased to write an introduction to the book, especially since it was initially his original concept.

Once the book was in the process of achieving the physical reality of publication, I sent Ivan a check for $200 as a thank you for writing the introduction. Ivan had not requested any kind of honorarium and had written the piece completely out of friendship.

164

I will cherish always the memory of his telephone call expressing his surprise and his thanks: "My boy, this will go toward the publication of our newsletter for the Society for the Investigation of the Unexplained. The others were just shuffling around and talking about it, but when I told them the boy from Iowa had just kicked in two hundred bucks, the others are reaching into their pockets and we will have a publication."

Two hundred dollars went much farther in 1966 than it would toward the publication of any newsletter today, and I was so very pleased that my "donation" had jump-started what would become *Pursuit*.

My agent declared 1966 the year of my publishing birth. *Strange Guests* was published and went into many printings. *Strangers from the Skies,* a collection of UFO accounts, was released shortly before Dr. J. Allen Hynek made his famous "swamp gas" analysis regarding the Michigan sightings that had made national headlines, and the book was catapulted onto the paperback bestseller lists just two weeks after publication. *ESP: Your Sixth Sense* became a textbook on college and high school levels and was even adapted for junior high classes, complete with workbook. *Valentino* was launched with unprecedented fanfare for an original paperback – full-page magazine ads, billboards, and radio spots on the CBS network, and was made into a motion picture by British director Ken Russell, starring Rudolf Nureyev as the Great Lover.

Ivan, Alma, and I maintained close contact by letter and telephone. I was distressed to learn that Alma's illness was terminal, but her late night calls "just to talk" were never filled with regrets, only with affection and optimism.

Then very late one night in 1968 came the call from Ivan that was filled with unrestrained excitement. "We've got it, my boy," he began. "We have found what I have searched for nearly all of my life. We have found proof of Yeti, the abominable snowman."

Ivan was obviously speaking from an outdoor pay phone. The wind was howling in the background, and I was uncertain that I had heard him correctly.

"Heuvelmans and I are 'way up north in Minnesota," Ivan said. "We've actually seen one frozen in ice. It's the real thing, my boy. We've got one to convince the skeptics."

And then there was so much static on the line that Ivan said he would call later with more details of what could be one of the most important scientific finds of the century.

The discovery that Sanderson and Heuvelmans had initially believed would confound the skeptics we now know as "Bozo," the "Iceman," the creature frozen in a block of ice that was being displayed by Frank Hansen. Bozo had obviously been shot and killed by someone, but Hansen denied having pulled the trigger, especially when it was suggested that the frozen corpse might be more human than animal. The story of Bozo became extremely complicated and controversial, amidst accusations that Ivan and Bernard Heuvelmans had been hoaxed by a conman who had shown them a rubber dummy with rotting meat beneath the display case to create the smell of putrefying flesh. Ivan would insist that the Bozo later examined by other experts had been switched and was not the authentic cadaver that he and Heuvelmans had originally been shown by Hansen.

Ivan and I continued to keep in touch over the years, but Alma's death, the controversy over the Iceman, and his own abdominal cancer made the calls and letters less frequent. In 1972, Ivan called and asked if I could help with a financial contribution to get an issue of *Pursuit* off the printing press. I was glad that I was able to do so, for Ivan passed into the Great Unknown on my birthday, February 19, 1973.

Brad Steiger
Venture, Iowa
July 29, 2006

Want more poltergeists?

Don't miss D. Scott Rogo's stunning autobiographical account of his search to witness and document this rare phenomenon.

On the Track of the
Poltergeist

D. Scott Rogo

Anomalist Books
anomalistbooks.com
ISBN: 193366505X
US $14.00/UK £9.00

9 781933 665177